ARE YOU FINANCIALLY CHECKMATE?

ARE YOU FINANCIALLY CHECKMATE?

You Live in an Economic Culture Designed to Keep You Broke. Discover How to Take Control and Free Yourself from Financial Bondage.

Tom Graneau, Sr.

To order additional copies of this book, contact:
Publish Writers Inc.
1-800-247-6553
www.publishwriters.com
Orders@publishwriters.com

10700-pw

CONTENTS

PART I
The Problem

Financially Busted 17
CHAPTER 1: The Personal Image 19
CHAPTER 2: The Undisputed Trail 25
CHAPTER 3: The Retirement Fantasy 36
CHAPTER 4: A Snapshot of the Emotional State
                        of Most Americans 47
CHAPTER 5: A Cultural Path to a Predictable Outcome................... 60

PART II
Causes of the Problem

Seven (7) Cultural Traps Designed to Keep You Broke 80
CHAPTER 6: Autoculture Kids, Youth and Money............................84
CHAPTER 7: Autoculture Beliefs, Values and Money........................93
CHAPTER 8: Autoculture Education 105
CHAPTER 9: Autoculture Jobs 122
CHAPTER 10: Autoculture Taxation.. 137
CHAPTER 11: Autoculture Credit and Debt 146
CHAPTER 12: Autoculture Economy.. 158

PART III
Solutions to the Problem

How to Master the Money Game to Win 171
CHAPTER 13: The Terms of Life 174
CHAPTER 14: Two Noteworthy Attributes of Money........................ 189
CHAPTER 15: The Five Functions of Money.................................... 196
CHAPTER 16: Money in Action... 203
CHAPTER 17: Winning the Money Game 231

To my daughter, **Sandra Graneau,**
and son **Thomas Graneau Jr.,** both of whom are
dreamers in their own rights.

Special thanks to

My mother, **Agnes Graneau**, who brought me to the
greatest country in the world (the United States of America) at a
young age.

To my adopted father, **David Chapman**, who molded, educated,
and led me into manhood.

To my loving wife, **Sharon Sanders-Graneau**, who supported me
throughout this entire project.

And special, special thanks to

God Almighty who makes all things possible

PREFACE

One of the happiest times of my life was the day I left the Caribbean and immigrated to the United States. At seventeen years old, I had no clue what that meant, but I was excited about the move. More so, I trusted my mother, a woman who was totally motivated to create a better life for herself and her children.

When I arrived in the United States, I was somewhat disappointed. There was no gold on the streets, like many people who come here expect to see. Neither was anything given to us freely. The reality was, we had to start building a new life from scratch, like most people who immigrate to this country.

Looking back, coming to America was the best thing that could have happened to me not only in terms of financial opportunities but also in terms of personal development. I was extremely shy, desperately lacking in mannerism, void of social discipline, and, most importantly, hollow in knowledge.

Strangely enough, none of these personal deficiencies bothered me in my old environment. I was doing fine until I came to this country. Suddenly, I became aware of my problems, and I didn't like what I saw.

The biggest issue, of course, was my lack of education. When I left the islands at age seventeen, I couldn't read or write. I had missed roughly 95 percent of my school period as a child and teenager, much of which had to do with family complications and my personal attitude about school. At age fifteen, my school window was closed entirely. This is hard to imagine because in so many ways I was still a child. But back then, if a teenager hadn't achieved a certain level in school, he or she was permanently expelled as a hopeless case. As a result, I had given up hope of ever going back to school.

After two years in the United States, my attitude about school had changed. My mind was hungry for knowledge, and I became obsessed with the idea of learning. But because I was nineteen years old, the road to my goal wasn't going to be easy. My age and educational level were on opposite ends of the pole. I was old enough to be a high school graduate yet had the education of a first grader.

In time, divine providence broke down the barriers and set me free. Some concerned friends came to my rescue and began creating an avenue by which I could get an education. In a matter of months, I was admitted to a private school. There, I was placed in a private room to start my education with second-grade classroom material. Two years later, I received a ninth-grade certificate and pursued a high school diploma in a separate school. The rest, of course, is history.

At twenty-four years old, I got married and started providing for a family, a duty I considered a privilege. But with each passing paycheck, I became increasingly concerned about my financial situation. Frankly, after years of working, I realized that I was going nowhere fast. After spending my entire paychecks on essentials for the home, like most Americans, I resorted to borrowing additional funds on credit cards to supplement my lifestyle, a habit that got increasingly worse with time.

In public, my family and I looked fine, except deep down, I felt uneasy about my financial situation. As my debt increased, I became more worried that something bad would eventually happen down the road. I had no money saved for emergencies, my family's *needs* and *wants* kept increasing, the prices of goods also kept increasing, retirement planning remained a distant concern, and my income stayed flat except for annual raises, which made little or no difference.

My worse fear came when I lost the job that I depended on for years. My income suddenly stopped, and my world started to crumble. After months of looking for work in a sluggish economy, I went from making roughly $25 an hour down to $6 an hour.

Needless to say, things got ugly. With debt up to my eyeballs, I had a difficult time holding everything together. My house went into foreclosure proceedings, and collectors started hounding me for monthly payments. After months of struggling with this situation, I decided to file bankruptcy and start over.

Today, I'm a financial counselor, planner, and educator. I like what I do because I get a tremendous amount of satisfaction in helping others avoid the economic traps that are laid before them. But sadly, too many people have been caught in the jaws of debt and have succumbed to the fatal bite. Worse, many more are on the verge of falling into the same trap. Moreover, I'm overwhelmed by people's financial misconceptions, ignorance, confusion, fear, and uncertainty. The truth is, millions of Americans are trapped in a life of financial anguish, a life where people endure pain quietly as a result of excessive debt and an inadequate supply of money. In this situation, survival is nothing more than a month-by-month ordeal, a situation most people would like to change. Yet in public, we pretend that everything is under control.

From the outside looking in, the streets of America are paved with gold. But it's funny how quickly the gold and glitter disappear as soon as one arrives in this country. Everything suddenly takes on a different view, changing imagination into reality. It's also interesting to note that the majority of people who live here have never seen the gold. To them, it doesn't exist.

Nevertheless, America is rich in gold, but the gold is not necessarily the type that is stored in the vaults of the Federal Reserve banks. No, the type that I speak of has more value. This country is truly the land of the free and the brave, one with limitless opportunities visible to only those who are willing to search for them. Yet when you look closely, few people have taken advantage of its bounties. Instead, the majority of us struggle to survive. Why?

For me, the light bulb came on late. Sitting in a university classroom week after week, trying to earn a degree, I came to realize that my financial problems were all too common. I heard some instructors or professors whine about their dismal financial conditions. The fact that some of them had more than one job suggested that they needed the money to make ends meet. Additionally, it seemed like the entire student body, many of which were working adults, were borrowing money to pay for their college degrees. I was no exception. In fact, that's the only means by which I could put myself through school because I was broke.

The irony was too obvious, however. The closer we got to receiving the college degree, the heavier the debt load became. And seemingly, every week, different people would start groaning under the heavy burden of debt. Many of my fellow students, including me, had accumulated in excess of $60,000 in student loans by graduation, an amount that would take years to pay.

It was then I became aware of the fact that this problem was bigger than most people realize, one that was rooted deep in our culture, causing most people to get financially sick. As a result, I decided to address the issue head on.

But the task wasn't going to be easy. First, I realized that there are thousands of books on the market addressing various aspects of finance.

One can find a book on literally any phase of finance, starting from basic budgeting to investments. The Internet—as well as magazines, newspapers, televisions, and radios—is loaded with data on the subject. So the problem is not a lack of financial information. Most people are aware of the fact that it's a good idea to save and invest money. Yet few take the opportunity to do so.

Second, this problem isn't a superficial concern that can be dissipated overnight. Instead, it's rooted deep in our culture and has woven itself within the fabric of lives. Frankly, it's in the heart of our economic system itself, something that will probably take time to undo. Much of the core issues deal directly with our way of life. Most of which are personal, highly private, and sensitive.

This book is by no means "the" comprehensive solution on the subject of finance. But it's the only book of its kind. The topic of finance is presented in ways that you haven't seen or heard before. It provides insights into the root problem, showing you how to undo or prevent the financial quagmire most of us experience daily.

Yet the attempt here is not to demean or criticize anyone's personal situations but rather to broach a national problem on a personal level. I am convinced that if there has to be changes in our personal financial lives—solutions that will alleviate the pain—we need to understand the problem from the root. It is only then we can experience fundamental change on this subject.

But be advised, the message may not be comfortable for some people. One of the reasons is because most people would like to be told that they're doing well even when reality proves otherwise. This book takes a different approach. The truth is, you may find the information to be direct and poignant for a good reason. Changes occur only when we face the truth head-on and deal with it. Otherwise, we'll keep kidding ourselves year after year, dreaming and hoping for change that may never come.

On the other hand, if you desire to see changes in your financial life, this book will provide the answers you need.

"The value of money is that with it we can tell any man to go to the devil. It is the sixth sense which enables you to enjoy the other five."

W. SOMERSET MAUGHAM (1874-1965).

Of Human Bondage, 51, 1915.

Are You Financially Checkmate?

You live in an economic culture designed to keep you broke. Discover how to take control and free yourself from financial bondage.

PART I
The Problem

"There are more important things than money—the only trouble is that they all cost money."

LOUIS A. SAFIAN.

Comp., *The Book of Updated Proverbs, 7, 1967.*

FINANCIALLY BUSTED

Unusual aches and pains in the body generally signal one thing: something is wrong. Granted, the problem may not be serious. It could be a simple prick in the finger, a common headache, or a sprained ankle. But whatever it is, our brain has the capacity to pinpoint the exact location and the intensity of the pain.

Generally speaking, small aches and pains pose no major threat to life. In fact, under certain conditions, they can be treated with over-the-counter medications. However, most unusual aches and pains require the expert diagnosis of a doctor, a general practitioner, or a specialist.

The worse approach to handling any type of discomfort in the body is to ignore it. By pretending it doesn't exist, the problem is likely to get worse. In which case, we become personally responsible for any additional complications caused by the original problem.

Yet this type of behavior is common. The idea is that as long as the soreness is tolerable, we remain hopeful that the body's healing mechanisms will take over and eventually cure the hurt. But you and I know that's not always possible, especially if the cause of the illness remains unknown.

There is another side to this analogy. All physical or biological ailments do not come with pain. Some grow slowly and painlessly. These are the worse kinds because the symptoms are neither seen nor felt during the developmental stages. Then suddenly, an emergency condition exists, prompting immediate action.

Financial maladies are no different. Monthly, the majority of us struggle with financial ailments. The paycheck-to-paycheck ordeal makes it difficult to adequately meet all our financial responsibilities and allow us the flexibility to plan successfully for the future. For the most part, we realize that the problem exists, but we ignore the symptoms. Our hope is that the shortage of cash will eventually get resolved. Meanwhile, the growing *needs* and *wants* in our lives never cease, causing us to keep yearning for additional money that never seems to come easily.

Occasionally, we single-handedly try to resolve the cash flow problem. Some of us seek jobs with higher pay, and others hold two or three jobs at a time—an admirable feat, to say the least. The attempt, of course, is to infuse additional cash into the equation. However, since the majority of us lack the fundamentals of economics and finance, we simply aggravate the problem with time. Hence, year after year, our financial complexities grow worse: less savings, less investments, more debt, more bankruptcies, more confusion, and more pain.

For the most part, we try to keep our financial calamity under control by patching up the problems. We hate to admit the fact that our situation isn't as rosy as we make it to be. What we fail to understand is that the root of our financial ailment lies deep in the very culture we embrace. And unless the root cause is understood, tackled, and changed, the problem will persist.

CHAPTER 1

The Personal Image

One of the fascinating things about the game of chess is that a good player has the ability to corner the opponent into a stalemate position—an immobilized, non-negotiating situation. It's also possible for a player to allow an opponent to dominate the game because of bad moves. Either way, if one player is unfamiliar with the rules of chess, the person will keep losing to the opponent, a condition known as *checkmate*. Once a player has been checkmated, the person has no other choice but to admit defeat and start the game over again, presuming that he or she has the opportunity to do so.

As you can tell, this book is not about playing chess but rather about personal finance—life and money. But believe it or not, in principle, there are huge similarities between the game of chess and the use of money. Each time we handle money (big or small), we are, in fact, playing a financial chess game with the economy. How well we do in the end depends heavily on our financial knowledge.

Unfortunately, because most of us lack the financial insight necessary to win the money game, we place ourselves at a disadvantage with people who know the rules. For this reason, we get *Financially Checkmated* without truly understanding how it happened.

For example, if I become acquainted with you and during our conversation ask, "How are you doing financially?" you would unequivocally respond by saying, "Fine." Of course, your reply would be canned and automatic because that's the way we've been groomed to respond on this topic. The reasons are simple: (1) you may think that I'm out of place to ask you such a question, (2) you may not have the desire to discuss the topic with me, (3) you may not be forthcoming if you say something about it, and (4) you may be totally embarrassed to admit that you're not doing as well as you should. In any case, it is certainly your privilege to be private about your financial situation.

But based on cultural economic habits, if you're not part of the 10 percent of people holding the majority of the wealth in this country, you're broke.

This broke condition doesn't necessarily mean that you have no income, although it's possible. In that case, you would be destitute. But more specifically, being broke means a financial state in which there is an established source of income—in some situations, a lot of it. Yet at the end of each month, you find yourself penniless. It also means having a sense that you're aging quickly and have little or no money put away for retirement. Worse, you have no idea how much money you'll need for retirement. Also, being broke is knowing that you could lose your home, your car(s), and your other valuable possessions in approximately three months or less as a result of losing your job—a sobering thought.

On the surface, your situation doesn't appear to be alarming. In fact, by popular standards, you appear to be doing well. You may have a bachelor's degree, a master's degree, or even a doctorate degree from a prestigious college or university. It may be that your education has paved the way for a perfect career, one that demands the skills of someone who's organized, proficient, and committed. You fit the role nicely. Also, you may be at the peak of your career and making a lot of money. Consequently, your income has provided you the opportunity to live in a beautiful home, drive an expensive car, and associate with people of status. Yet all the money you make slips through your fingers each month, leaving you broke year after year.

If this description doesn't fit your profile exactly, that's okay. It could be that all you have is a high-school diploma instead of a degree. You live in an average house or an apartment, you drive an average car, and you hold a comparable job to your education. Even so, within your means, you still find yourself struggling with your finances month after month, with not enough money to make ends meet.

Here, too, you appear to be doing fine in public. You dress well, you smell good, you talk big, and you give the impression that everything is under control. Privately, however, your real situation keeps you nervous. You're aging, you have very little savings or investments, and all your income vanishes each month.

In your condition, it's not unusual to feel that you're the only one experiencing financial hardship. Frankly, when life gets us down, it's only natural to feel lonely, powerless, and isolated. In moments like these, everyone else appears to be doing better in comparison. In other words, when you're broke, it's easy to see shoppers filling American malls, buying ceaselessly. Meanwhile, you cringe with frustration, hoping that your situation will soon end so you, too, can do the same thing.

But don't be fooled; the image you see is false. Those who know the truth see a different picture, one of which people remain cash poor while they borrow money to survive. As a result, they usually become *economic casualties* due to excessive debt. They keep borrowing until they experience embarrassing financial hardships such as bankruptcy, fore-closures, repossessions, and ultimately, a tarnished credit history. When these things happen, those involved are considered high-risk and, more often than not, they're treated as second-class citizens.

This situation is appalling when you consider the fact that America is the most affluent country in the world. Yet so many of us struggle with our finances. Could it be that we spend too much money on nothing? Is it because some of us don't make enough money? Are we accumulating too much personal debt? Or is it because most of us simply lack the basic concepts of personal finance and economics?

If your answer is "yes" to all of the above, you would be partially right. The interesting thing is, most Americans would agree with you. The fact is, the majority of us realize that there's something fundamentally wrong with the way we conduct business. But for many of us, the problem is too big to tackle. Instead of viewing it as an individual's issue desperately needing attention, we see it as a group issue, putting the responsibility on the masses. Doing so not only turns the problem into a distant, unfixable mess, but it also as allows us freedom to continue spending without guilt or interruption.

This kind of thinking is irresponsible. It creates additional problems. First, it gives us an opportunity to hide our personal financial issues until they get beyond our capacity to handle. Second, it perpetuates the false pretense seen in the marketplace every day: a habit of continued shopping and buying even when our cash has run out.

But no matter how we try to blame the masses for our financial incompetence, the impact is ultimately felt by the individual, the single most valued unit of any culture. It is in the home that the problem persists: the impulsive shopping habit, the excessive spending, the lack of savings, and the constant yearning for additional money.

To shed light on some of the specific individual issues, consider the following points:

- You may be bringing home a lot of money, yet you find yourself wishing you had a few more dollars to cover all of your financial responsibilities at the end of each month. Your budget (if you have one) is simply too tight. On the other hand, coming up with the extra money may not be easy. To do so, you may have to give up evening school or sacrifice your weekends for a second or third job. None of these options are pleasant. Yet something must be done because your situation is getting worse.

- If you own a house, chances are you have a first, second, or even a third mortgage on the property. In that case, you may have used the equity in the home to improve the property, pay for college education, pay off credit card debts, or go on a vacation. What's more, you may have pulled more equity from the property than it's worth, a 125 percent loan to value for instance. In the back of your mind, you know these mortgages will never get paid unless you win the lottery. But for now, you take comfort in the fact that you can at least keep up with the monthly payments and have a place to call home.

- Your 401(k) plan is your only savings or investment because you haven't had the money or discipline to save any other way. But although you were told that this investment is designed for retirement, you may have dipped into it once or twice for things like a down payment on house, the purchase of a vehicle, college tuition, or even a vacation. Consequently, this has diminished the strength and value of your retirement plan.

- You may have tried your luck on Wall Street and considered yourself an investor. But you gamble by speculating market changes before you make your move. The reason? You lack the skill, experience, and money to be comfortable in the market. So instead of making money, you gradually lose the grip on your investment.

- You know that it's important to save a portion of your earnings. Yet you have trouble doing so. Consequently, you have no money set aside for emergencies, and the situation bothers you. All the years you've worked have proven to be nothing more than simply making enough money to survive. Worse, you've allowed your emotions to override your judgment, causing you to keep spending every dollar you make.

- You have several credit cards, most of which have reached their limits. You've been paying the 2 or 3 percent minimum payment. Yet the balances keep rising. You're frustrated by watching your hard-earned money being sucked away by interest payments. But you feel helpless as you think of ways to get out from under the financial burden. Meanwhile, you have no choice but to stay in the good graces of the credit card companies. Otherwise, they may ruin your credit history, making life even more difficult for you in the future.

- It could be that you've already filed bankruptcy due to excessive debt or loss of income. The experience was real and painful. As a result, you promised your family that you would do everything possible to avoid repeating the problem in the future. It's roughly four years later, and you've accumulated additional debt that threatens to take you down the same path. But this time, you're stuck because legally bankruptcy is not option.

- If you are a college graduate, chances are, you've accumulated student loans. But making payments on them has become less of a priority because of other financial demands. Besides, you believe that these loans will be with you for the rest of your life, so why sweat it?

- If you have children, you are worried about college expenses. Over the years, you've been told that your children's college fund should be one of your highest priorities.But now, college enrollment is right around the corner, and you're not prepared to handle that responsibility.

- When the experts say that the economy is doing well, you wonder who has the money because you're still broke. It's true that you may have had a promotion and have gotten a raise or two, but the extra money has simply disappeared.

- You've heard that Social Security is an unreliable source of retirement income. Yet your lack of financial planning has left you no choice but to rely on the program. You and millions more will be looking for a check from the Social Security Administration for roughly $970 a month (single) or roughly $11,640 a year.

At first, you may not see any danger associated with these issues because most of them are common to our way of life. But as you read further, you'll see how these events have been used to control and manipulate your financial outcome, thus, keeping you broke.

If you're not completely happy with your financial outcome, my guess is that this is not the result you expected at this stage in your life. I would further assume that you may have spent a lot of time and money for higher education and training in order to succeed financially. If this is true, your list of questions could be quite long.

For example, you may be wondering:

- Why am I still broke after years of working?
- Why has it been so difficult to save or invest part of my earnings?
- When I finally put some money in savings, why do I find it so easy to dip into the funds?
- Why am I in debt and continue to be in debt in spite of my efforts to prevent it?
- Are other people struggling as much or experiencing the same types of financial hardships?

In your case, these questions are valid. What's more is that every financially unstable American should be asking the same thing. Unfortunately, most of these questions don't surface until later in life, after years and years of working fruitlessly.

One of the main reasons is because much of what we've discussed so far has become the standard by which we do things, making it difficult to spot and solve financial problems early. For example, if most of us are told that we're making financial progress when we purchase items on credit, the practice itself becomes the standard. When viewed this way, there is no problem because most people are doing the same thing. Meanwhile, most of us go through life creating false success.

CHAPTER 2

The Undisputed Trail

We, as a group, have learned to master the art of covering our personal financial deficiencies. For as much as we say and do, our financial affairs remain intimately private. In addition to staying mum on the subject, we've learned to use props such as educational accomplishments and job titles to hide the truth. For example, one could easily think or say that because of our college education or job titles, no one dare thinks that we are broke and in debt. Yet for those who know the difference, personal accomplishments have little to do with financial success.

Another way we try to disguise the truth is by purchasing expensive items. Possessions such as houses, cars, and boats, give the appearance that one is doing well financially. But again, much of it could be smoke and mirrors. Generally, the lifestyle we create is done through credit, leaving our situation wide open for future problems. The image eventually cracks under pressure, revealing the real truth about our financial conditions—secrets we would rather hide if we could.

For obvious reasons, we have the right to conceal our financial information—personal protection, for one—in which case, the Privacy Act affords us the right to do so. Our credit history: though it may contain some damaging remarks, the content is disclosed only to those who have a need to know.

But despite that fact that we try to keep a tight lid on our personal financial conditions, there are other ways of telling how well we're doing as a group. The fact is, as we move ahead from year to year, we leave trails behind us depicting our behavior. These trails provide clues not only about events of the past, but also what lies ahead for us financially. In other words, we're financially predictable.

The reality is, we're in the habit of building our empires on credit. And as such, our lifestyle remains tenuous. Like a tamed lion with a wild nature, the volatility of credit does eventually expose the truth about our financial situations in spite of our efforts to conceal them.

Household Debt

When it comes to accumulating debt, Americans have no trouble doing it fast. Most of us are experts in that department because we use the system every day to buy possessions.

But having experienced or seen the devastation brought about by excess debt, one would think that the potential risks would be enough to diminish or halt our appetite for credit. But that's not the case. When the shopping impulse flares up, if credit is the only means by which we're able to satisfy our wants, we use it. As a result, it has become the most popular way by which we obtain the things we desire. Today, our personal debt load is staggering. Government figures show that Americans are piling up debt with little or no regard for consequential fallback. In a twelve-year period, we increased household debt by 141 percent from $3.6 trillion in 1990 to $8.7 trillion in 2002 (see figure 2.1).

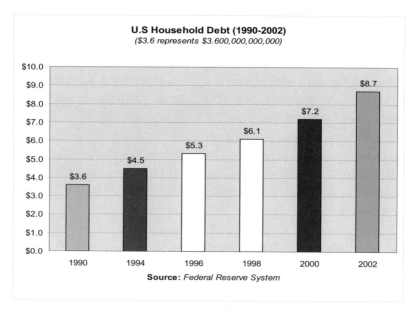

Fig 2.1

Personal Savings

As household debt rises, one should expect a corresponding drop in personal savings, which is exactly what's happening. Although the two actions are independent of each other, the amount of money one saves depends heavily on the availability of cash. Therefore, when excessive cash is predisposed for debt payment, less of it becomes available for basic necessities and personal savings.

The following chart provides an example in such a case. Based on government numbers, personal gross savings dropped from $334 billion in 1990 to negative $ 3.9 billion in 2002 (see figure 2.2).

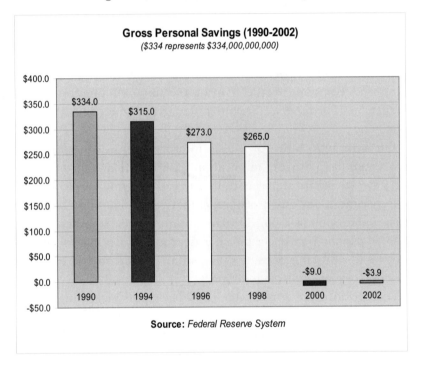

Fig 2.2

As you can see, the savings rate on disposable income reveals a steady decline into the negative region of the chart within the same period of escalating debt. Information from a different source reflects a similar trend (see figure 2.3).

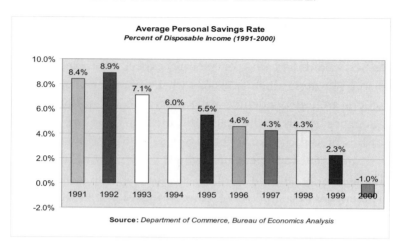

Fig.2.3

Keep in mind that personal savings is a tricky term that's usually mis-understood. For many people, it means the amount money one saves for emergencies. For others, it includes emergency funds plus Wall Street investments.

But although both of these interpretations are correct, the government has a broader implication. To Uncle Sam, personal savings covers everything from pretax dollars to post tax dollars. According to the Department of Commerce, it includes a compilation of money in a pension plan such as a 401(k) plan; an individual retirement account (IRA); stocks and bonds; certificate of deposits; money market accounts; savings and checking accounts; and money given to friends, family, charitable organizations, and others.

Furthermore, the government considered personal savings to mean any money left over after subtracting meaningful expenses from in-come. Meaningful expenses include money spent for food, housing, clothing, medicine, transportation, utilities, and so on. It also includes interest payments on personal loans and credit cards. Additionally, it takes into consideration money contributed to Social Security insur-ance and taxes.

So, if you haven't spent your entire paycheck on meaningful ex-penses, according to the government, you have money in savings even though your bank account might be empty. Yet by it's own definition, the same government admits that personal savings is seriously eroding each year.

The Credit Card Dust

You've seen the numbers for household debt and personal savings, the negative implication of which is irrefutable. Our debt balances keep escalating into trillions of dollars while our savings plummet into billions.

If these two charts showed equal alignments, the situation wouldn't be too bad. One could argue that although we're not saving money, our debt load is remaining flat. But these two issues are opposites, creating a double negative. As debt rises, personal savings keep dropping.

One of the biggest contributing factors associated with the steady rise of debt is the credit card. This tool is responsible for getting more Americans in financial trouble than anything else. Yet the number of credit card holders keeps rising. According to the U.S. Census Bureau, 163 million Americans carry credit cards in their wallets and purses, and this number is expected to climb to 173 million people by the end of 2005 (see figure 2.4). Other surveys show the current number as high as 185 million people.

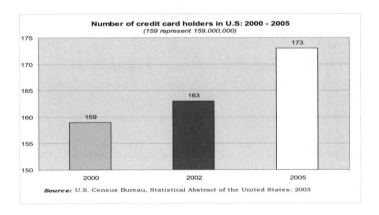

Fig. 2.4

The trend is clear. One can easily speculate that before the gap between debt and savings narrows, it will get wider. Another thing that's also obvious is that the credit card system is here to stay, and people intend to use it. The equation is simple: as people become more and more cash depleted, the more they'll rely on borrowed money to continue doing business.

And why not? The system appears to make life easier for millions of people. It provides total convenience in every situation. And just to be sure that we always have access to money, some of us carry more than one card. In fact, the average American carries 12.1 credit cards at any given time. According to 2002 government figures, there are 1.4 billion active credit card accounts in the United States, a number that is projected to rise by the end of 2005 (see figure 2.5).

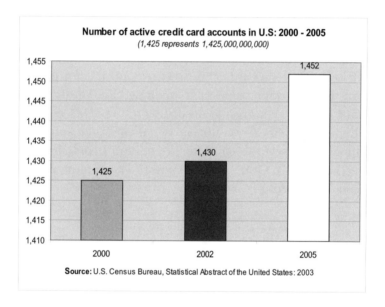

Fig. 2.5

If you're surprised by the vast number of active credit card accounts in this country, you may be one of the individuals who has no more than two or three accounts. Some of my clients carried as many as twenty different credit cards at one time, most of which had large balances.

Given the number of active credit card accounts, the volume of spending shouldn't be surprising either. In fact, there's a direct correlation to the number of cards people carry and the amount of spending they do. The more ways they have to tap into new money, the more they spend. The *2002 Statistical Abstract of the United States* shows that credit card holders spent in excess of $1.4 trillion in 2000. And by the end of 2005, this figure will have climbed to $2 trillion (see figure 2.6).

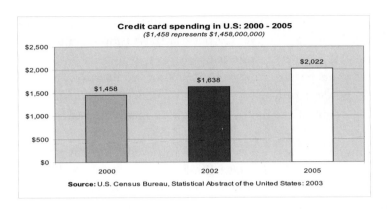

Fig. 2.6

There is another phenomenon associated with the credit card system: once a card is issued to a consumer, it is usually put to use immediately. The reasons are mostly psychological. The client gets inspired by having access to new money, feels privileged to be associated with a well-established credit card company, and gets a sense of satisfaction through shopping while contributing to the economy.

Notwithstanding, credit card users almost never win the credit game. Excessive spending usually creates high debt balances, which makes it nearly impossible to pay in full. As such, the odds are stacked against them. For instance, outstanding consumer credit card balances in 2000 capped at $680 billion. This number is expected to rise as high as $922 billion by the end of 2005 (see figure 2.7).

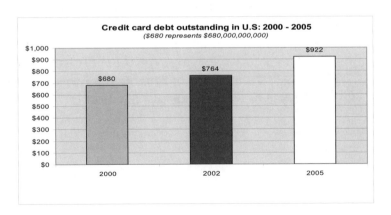

Fig. 2.7

For those who understand the magnitude of these figures, the reality is appalling. For the average person, these numbers mean nothing. In a nutshell, each year, Americans carry an average of $8,562 in credit card debt and pay an average of $1,000 in credit card interest. Moreover, 60 percent of active credit card balances go unpaid each year, and 48 percent of cardholders struggle to maintain just the minimum payments.

Strangely enough, every time we use credit, we have a legitimate reason for doing so. At least, we think we do. A recent poll showed that 60 percent of U.S. consumers use their credit cards for one of these reasons: (1) living above their means, (2) not making enough money, (3) ease and convenience of credit, and (4) emergency spending.

For some of us, the issue comes down to emotions or no reason at all. We simply react and think later. This type of behavior is unhealthy when it comes to spending money. It usually leads to other issues such as "buyer's remorse." One of my clients humbly admitted that she consistently overspends. "Buying," she said, "is therapeutic until I walk away. When I get home, I usually feel guilty and end up taking more than half of the items back to the store."

There are other factors in the equation that are worth considering. There are those who feel that when they find a bargain, it's time to stock. So they peel out their credit cards and shop like tomorrow may never come. Unfortunately, this group is somewhat confused. They think they're getting a deal when, in fact, they'll end up spending twice as much for the items.

For example, assume you purchased discounted items in the amount of $5,000 on one credit card, and the annual percentage rate (APR) was 20 percent. If you pay the minimum 2 percent monthly payment, it will take a little more than nine (9) years to pay off the entire balance. In the end, you will have paid a grand total of $10,840 in principal and interest, $5,840 of which will be interest only (see figure 2.8).

APR	2% Mon. Pmt	Loan Amt	No. of Yrs	Interest Paid	Total Amt Paid
8%	$100	$5000	5.2	$1,102	$6,102
10%	$100	$5000	5.5	$1,494	$6,494
12%	$100	$5000	5.10	$1,966	$6,966
14%	$100	$5000	6.4	$2,547	$7,547
16%	$100	$5000	6.11	$3,294	$8,294
18%	$100	$5000	7.10	$4,311	$9,311
19%	$100	$5000	8.4	$4,985	$9,985
20%	**$100**	**$5,000**	**9.1**	**$5,840**	**$10,840**
21%	$100	$5000	10.0	$6,986	$11,986
22%	$100	$5000	11.5	$8,678	$13,678

Fig. 2.8

Did you save? Of course not. You thought that you were getting a great deal, but that's not the case at all. The evidence proves otherwise.

The Bankruptcy Impact

Bankruptcy is a procedure few people want to undertake. In addition to having one's credit history tarnished, bankruptcy has an immoral undertone that makes people feel uncomfortable. As a result, those who find themselves in a bankrupt situation usually hesitate prior to making a decision. And when they file, though they feel somewhat relieved of the financial burden, they're generally remorseful and humble about the experience.

So reasonably, it's fair to assume that people who file bankruptcy have no intention of doing so initially. They simply go about living their lives without the thought of filing. On the other hand, those who carelessly spend on credit thinking that they can escape bankruptcy and other forms of financial hardships are simply fooling themselves. Using credit is like playing with fire. You're likely to get burned if the blaze gets too hot.

Such is the case here. Public records show that millions of debt-laden Americans have filed bankruptcy in recent years. Starting from 1980, bankruptcy has risen well above 400 percent. And although the trend dipped slightly in 2000, the numbers are consistently rising. More than 1.5 million people filed Chapter 7 and Chapter 13 bankruptcy in 2002 (see figure 2.9).

Granted, excessive debt is not the only cause for bankruptcy. More than 40 percent of people who went into bankruptcy did so after a job loss, divorce, medical catastrophe, or a death in the family. But one files bankruptcy only when debt is present.

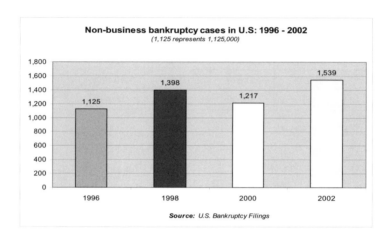

Fig. 2.9

And that's exactly the point. Because most of us carry huge amounts of debt each year, our lifestyles are predisposed to bankruptcy. One simple unfortunate circumstance requiring money can get the ball rolling in that direction. The formula is simple: *debt* on the house plus *debt* on the rest of our possessions minus emergency cash or good planning equals potential bankruptcy in case of a job loss, divorce, or any other unfortunate financial mishap. That's the equation, one that begs for financial wisdom and caution.

Another realistic component to the bankruptcy saga is this: when one goes into Chapter 7 bankruptcy, it may appear that the debt is gone. But in actuality, the cost lingers in the community for years. It gets distributed in bits and pieces to each one of us. Then, instead of one person bearing the responsibility for the debt, everyone pays a portion of it in higher cost of living.

So the next time you see your friend or neighbor pulling a credit card to make a purchase, it is more than a simple transaction. In addition to stirring up the economy and creating jobs, the same transaction becomes indirectly a potential threat to your livelihood. Since all of us are in this together, the action of everyone affects all of us. Therefore, when one accumulates debt and is unable to meet the financial obligation, we all get stuck with the bill, an extra burden none of us want.

More significantly, those of us who consistently use credit to create a lifestyle beyond our means are potentially destroying our long-term success. In addition to paying interest for the rest of our lives, we consistently live a life without cash, causing us to rely more and more on credit in the future.

So, for as much as we love to believe that our financial affairs are in order, the evidence we leave behind tells a different story. The truth is, we're a people deep in hock, wishing for the best each day.

CHAPTER 3

The Retirement Fantasy

None of us want to experience a bad ending in any situation. That includes getting to retirement age and living in poverty, or something close to it, for the rest of our lives. Yet, that's exactly what is going to happen for millions of Americans. Today, many of us are now realizing that our debt load is threatening our retirement outlook. Even the most naïve can tell that as we continue to create a lifestyle with credit, we're carving a predictable outcome for the future, the kind of life that most of us dread.

We see every day: retired parents, grandparents, friends, neighbors, and relatives who once thought that they were doing well with retirement preparation. Today, many of them are being forced to live on a low fixed income provided by the Social Security Administration, an amount limited to providing just basic necessities.

For those who are unaware of the condition of most Social Security income recipients, the picture is not rosy. Because of their fixed incomes, many of them experience financial inconvenience. For instance, because money is in short supply, most retirees have no choice but to keep working to supplement their Social Security incomes. Even then, they keep borrowing additional money (home-equity loans, for instance) just to make ends meet. And compared to those who are financially well-off, they receive less than the best of medical and dental services. Additionally, as a result of their cash depleted condition, they have no choice but to limit their fun and recreational activities which creates additional health problems.

The reality is, roughly 90 percent of current retirees depend on Social Security for more than 51 percent of their income. If this program wasn't available, one can only imagine an absolute deplorable condition in which to survive. Many would probably be homeless, others would be penniless, and yet some would rely entirely on charitable donations and other types of similar services.

For those of us who are still working, this is not the kind of outcome we look forward to. No, the retirement outlook we see is much more attractive. We expect a life of abundance, comfort, and pleasure, one with lots of time, money, and travel.

Yet millions of us are unknowingly falling into the same financial pit as our parents. Instead of a life of plenty, we'll end up with one of disappointment. The signs are there. *First,* it's evident that if we keep borrowing money and using the bulk of our present income for debt payment and other expense, it stands to reason that we'll have less cash for savings. *Second,* if we currently struggle from paycheck to paycheck without any major changes in behavior, the future will, undoubtedly, be more difficult to handle with less cash. *Third,* if time is our ally when investing, the longer we procrastinate some type of retirement program, the less money we will accumulate for the future. And *fourth,* if after investing in a 401 (k) plan or an IRA account and we consistently borrow from it for down payments on houses and children's education, less cash will be available for retirement.

So while it may be easy to anticipate a favorable retirement condition, it may not be as easy to create one. This is certainly true in our case. On one hand, we expect to live a blissful life in the sunset, but on the other hand, we make little or no preparation for it. Instead, our daily conduct proves that retirement planning remains an afterthought. When we must address the problem, we show our vulnerability—financial ignorance, lack of perceptive knowledge regarding the issue, and a state of helplessness. Yet we keep hoping that everything will magically fall into place at the right time.

Bet on Retirement

As certain as you're alive today, you can be sure that you're going to grow old. Not in the sense that you'll be looking forward to being old but, more importantly, in the way you will instinctively do everything you possibly can to extend your life. Additionally, nature and medical miracles will contribute in helping you stay alive longer.

Therefore, you will, more than likely, reach retirement age and beyond.

At that time, you will have hoped that during the course of your working years, you planned well enough to have options during retirement: having good medical care, finding time for relaxation, buying the things you want without the worry of money, and spending time with family and friends.

The question is, what kind of lifestyle will you have during retirement? My guess is that you're hoping that life will continue to be as you have it today or better. If that's the way you see it, I wish you the best. But be cautious. Because if you're not progressively planning and working to create that lifestyle, you are dreaming.

Condition of Current Retirees

Caution: The following information may be somewhat disturbing because it speaks of the negative aspects of current retirees. Nevertheless, a perceptive view on this subject is not only important but also crucial for the understanding of those who are not yet retired. First of all, no one is naïve enough to think that all retired Americans are struggling financially. There are many well-to-do people who live happy and comfortable lives in their sunset years. These individuals have all the money they need and the freedom to use it. They take extended vacations, spend time with grandchildren, pay for private doctors and nursing care, and make large charitable donations to groups of their choice. Furthermore, they pay no attention to the price tag when shopping for an item because the need for money is not a concern.

But most retires don't enjoy this type of lifestyle. Their conditions are poor. Today, only 30 percent of retired Americans say that they have enough money saved to last through retirement. The rest are relying solely on Social Security and Medicare for survival.

For these individuals, their futures are uncertain. Some are deeply concerned that Social Security and Medicare won't be around when they'll need it the most. Only 7 percent of current retirees feel that Social Security and Medicare will continue to provide benefits for as long as they need it. Furthermore, since the cost of medical expenses is consistently rising, only 31 percent have some assurance that they'll have enough money saved to cover medical costs.

Additionally, there are those who feel that retirement life is simply a day-by-day ordeal, one that's plagued with financial and health complications. Some individuals feel too sick to enjoy life and are too well to die. Some have described their situation as nothing more than a "miserable existence," one that seems to go on forever.

Another interesting point is this: not all current retirees who have stopped working did so because of age. There were other factors that came into the equation which forced them out of the work force. In fact, many of them retired because of situations beyond their control. Consider the following reasons:

- 41 percent retired due to health and disability complications
- 15 percent retired due to family crises
- 14 percent retired because of company problems (downsizing or shutdowns)
- 14 percent retired because of adequate financial resources
- 13 percent retired due to other work-related problems

Losing an income unwillingly is no fun, especially when there's little hope of earning another. Those who lose the ability to continue to work have no choice but to keep seeking income through other means, one of which is Social Security. Today, 65 percent of current retirees depend on Social Security for more than 51 percent of the their income, and 34 percent depend on it for more than 90 percent of their income. Viewed another way, more than 90 percent of current retirees rely on Social Security for at least 51 percent of their income, a figure quoted earlier.

If you're unfamiliar with Social Security distribution, the annual allotment may surprise you. In 2004, the maximum contribution for a single person was $11,640 up from $11,520 in 2003. For those who used to bring home roughly $35,000 a year while working, one can only imagine the change in lifestyle.

Today, however, the future of Social Security is extremely unstable. As more information becomes available, it appears that the system is about to collapse completely unless Congress takes action to stop it. Facts from the Social Security Administration suggest that projected Social Security tax will begin to decline rapidly by 2018. At which time, the system will provide for only 73 percent of scheduled benefits, leaving roughly 27 percent of people without income. According to the agency, for the program to remain solvent, it needs $3.5 trillion in today's money and generating interest at Treasury rates.

Seeing the danger ahead, Alan Greenspan, Chairman of the Federal Reserve Board, also commented about the program. As recently as February 2003, he put the public on notice by saying that recent estimates show that the Social Security System will be insolvent as early as 2020, unless Congress intervenes. How is that for reality?

The reasons for concern are simple and obvious. In 1950, for example, one Social Security recipient was being supported by sixteen contributing workers. But over the years, this number has gradually diminished to a dwindling 3.3 workers per recipient. By 2031, the number is expected to drop to 2 people.

Yet a bigger problem about Social Security looms at the horizon. In 2011, the baby boomer generation will be turning 65, and the majority of them will be depending on the program to survive. Additionally, the eighty-something population is one of the fastest-growing groups in this country. In 2000, eighty-five year olds accounted for 2 percent of the population. By 2050, the number is expected to increase to 5 percent, a whopping 19 million people, according to the U.S. Census Bureau. Most of these people will be relying on the system as their main source of income.

Never in the history of this country have we experienced such as an explosive growth in the older segment of our population. In one way, this speaks well for the advancement of medicine and technology. But this situation poses a danger to the economy and particularly, on the Social Security program. Simply put, the system will not be able to support everyone who depends on it unless Congress takes drastic steps to remedy the problem.

For those who understand the economic implication, this situation spells trouble. In cases where people live longer than planned, they usually end up depleting their savings and must depend entirely on Social Security. But in the event that the system collapses completely, the financial burden falls directly on relatives.

People who have the resources to care for parents and grandparents, the decision is simple. They usually place their elders in a nursing home and pay for the services. According to industry statistics, the cost ranges from $156 to $200 a day. Experts conclude that the annual cost could get as high as $120,000 or more. Yet, for those people, this solution is worth the money because it allows them to continue their lives with minimum interruptions. Today, roughly 2 million Americans are being cared for in nursing homes.

Caregivers who can't afford the cost of a nursing homes, however, the solution is more complicated. Their elders usually end up staying in the home. Today, 86 percent of baby boomers have selected to provide home care for their parents, a trend that's expected to grow with time. In fact, by 2011, American families will have more parents to care for than children.

This issue poses both a positive and a negative end. Psychologically, most people prefer spending their last days in the home with loved ones close by. The situation provides an opportunity for grandchildren to have continued relationships with grandparents, a huge social benefit for all involved. Additionally, it also creates an environment where everyone has a chance to experience the complete cycle of life, an irreplaceable experience particularly for grandchildren.

On the other hand, home care can be emotionally and financially draining. Since most caregivers must hold jobs to survive, the strain of providing care and meeting job demands eventually becomes a burden. Caregivers must make adjustments at work in order to give more attention to ailing parents. More than half of them usually request multiple leaves of absence or time off. And since Medicare and private health insurances do not pay for long-term home care, the financial responsibility usually falls on caregivers. As a result, in almost every caregiving situation, elders receive no more than adequate care.

Attitude of Current Workers

In light of all these negative messages, American workers remain positive about the future. Most of us maintain the attitude that our retirement will be never be as bad as the ones experienced by our parents. In fact, we're so confident that we look forward to retiring early. According to recent surveys, one out of three of us would like to retire at age fifty-five or younger, and two out of three are hoping to retire before age sixty-five.

Interestingly enough, the younger the people, the earlier they want to retire. Seventeen percent of preboomers, 29 percent of early boomers, and 38 percent of late boomers say they'd like to retire at age fifty-five or younger. Yet 51 percent of Generation X expresses the same desire.

For what it's worth, this positive outlook is good for the soul. People who remain hopeful in spite of difficult situations usually live longer than those with no hope. On the other hand, people who expect good endings need to be reminded that nothing good comes easy. They must put in the work to get the results they want.

But this is not happening. Surveys show that when it comes to retirement planning, Americans are simply dreaming about the future. While most of use would love to retire early, few of us are making plans to do so. Only 36 percent of American workers have actually tried to estimate the amount of money they'll need during retirement. Of the 36 percent who have done the research, only 23 percent can provide a solid answer when asked about retirement planning. In other words, roughly 77 percent of current workers have no idea how much money they'll need for retirement, discrediting the idea of early retirement.

Retirement Savings Preparation

Recent surveys have provided stunning information regarding savings for retirement. One survey showed that 69 percent of current workers claim to have saved a good amount of money for retirement. The amount varies from one group to the next. Consider the following:

- In the *preboomer* category (people who are more than sixty years old), 31 percent have saved over $100,000, 18 percent have stashed away $50,000 to $100,000, 32 percent have set aside $10,000 to $50,000, 8 percent have saved $10,000, and 11 percent have saved nothing.
- In the *early-boomer* camp (people who are more than fifty years old), 25 percent have saved $100,000, 19 percent have accumulated $50,000 to $100,000, 31 percent claim to have $10,000 to $50,000, 12 percent have $10,000, and 13 percent have nothing.
- In the *late-boomer* group (people who are more than forty years old), 20 percent have no savings, 24 percent have saved $10,000, 43 percent have put away $10,000 to $50,000, and 13 percent have saved $50,000 or more.

- In the *Generation X* camp (people in their late twenties), 28 percent have no money saved, 26 percent have accumulated less than $10,000, 33 percent have saved $10,000 to $50,000, and 13 percent have accumulated over $50,000.

If the surveys are true, this is clearly a step in the right direction. Everyone who has and continues to save toward a retirement program is obviously doing the right thing. In today's economy, it takes a great deal of effort and self-discipline to save money, since the urge to spend is always present.

The Issue of Enough

Considering the preceding numbers, one could say that current workers are making progress toward retirement savings. Yes. On the surface, that appears to be true. Any amount of money saved for this purpose is a step in the right direction.

However, the issue of enough money comes into question. One can easily be misled into thinking that any arbitrary amount of money saved for retirement is good enough, which is most likely the case in those examples. Otherwise, the following survey presents a contradiction in the behavior of workers regarding retirement savings. For example, seventy-eight percent of Americans believe to be financially ready for retirement. Yet we've saved only 12 percent of the required funds.

Another survey presents a similar situation. Experts agree that most of us are simply dreaming about the prospect of early retirement. Because while we are fantasizing about a good life in the future, roughly 71 percent of working adults have done little to prepare for retirement. And when the time comes, most of us, they say, won't be ready to retire.

Given these conflicting points of view, it is evident that most of us are confused about the issue of retirement. On one hand, financial experts agree that roughly 77 percent of the population lacks the ability to compute their retirement needs. Yet approximately the same number of people (78 percent) claim to be ready for retirement.

What's wrong with this picture? Are we kidding ourselves? That seems to be the case. The irony is, of course, we're deceiving no one except ourselves.

The fact is, a person who lacks the capacity to measure his or her financial retirement needs can easily get excited about $10,000 in a 401(k) plan or IRA account. In fact, $10,000 could be a huge sum of money for someone who is used to seeing less. Yet this amount is woefully inadequate for any type of future financial stability. The same is true for $20,000, $50,000, or even $100,000, especially when matched with fifteen, thirty, or even forty-five years of additional life after retirement. So for someone who is confused or lacks the knowledge to tell the difference, any amount of money saved toward retirement could be enough.

I recently met with a good friend of mine who is retiring in three years. Having saved roughly a $100,000 in a 401(k) plan, he felt proud of his success and wanted me to know about it. Sharing in his excitement, I took the opportunity to congratulate him for a job well done. Sparing his feelings, I held back any negative or disappointing comments, at least for the time being.

But needless to say, I saw potential problems ahead for my friend, things that are likely to happen in the not-so-distant future. For instance, the $100,000, which probably took him years to accumulate, could vanish in less than three years, leaving him stranded for the rest of his life. Assume, for example, that he needs roughly $3,000 a month to pay for things such as a mortgage, car payment, food, and so on, the money will last roughly three years and come to an end unless, of course, he subdues his lifestyle by cutting the monthly draws in half, which may or may not be easy. The money would last twice as long—six years instead of three.

My friend is not the only one in this predicament. Currently, over 50 million American workers have no job pensions. Yet the prospect of living solely on Social Security has gotten increasingly risky. According to financial experts, each of us will need a minimum of $30,000 a year during retirement just to break even. Most of the living expenses will be devoted primarily to medical costs. The current trend suggests that three in four people (75 percent) will need long-term medical care as we get older. This kind of outlook leaves us no choice but to prepare for the worse scenario and life could become unimaginably difficult.

If retirement planning and personal expectations are so far apart, one is left to wonder what's causing the early retirement fever. Are we expecting to retire and live comfortably without adequate financial resources? Of course not. We are Americans. The idea of having our cake and eating too is the way we see life regardless of how old we get.

So if we expect to live comfortably during retirement and are making little or no preparation for that phase of our lives, are we being influenced to believe a lie? It appears so. The advertising and entertainment media is doing a good job in creating false hope in Americans about retirement. The concept is simple. In words and pictures, the media conveys the idea that we need not worry about the future. The message is eat, drink, and be merry today, and the needs of the future will fall into place automatically. The communication is subtle: it's not surprising to see television images portraying older Americans having a ball. They live in luxurious centers, play golf whenever they want, and spend time in spas and saunas.

Seldom does the entertainment media show a situation where some retirees are plagued with financial problems, feelings of uselessness, poor health, and depression. Doing so would be too realistic and counterproductive to their mission. Instead, the idea is to encourage Americans to keep spending with little guilt about saving money for the future. We're being manipulated into thinking that saving money is a meaningless task—one that provides no short-term benefit. So why bother saving?

Reality Hits Home

As with everything else, reality is the best teacher. Time is beginning to expose the truth to many workers who, at one point, wished to retire early. Recent surveys indicate that early retirement hopefuls are faced with the choice of recanting their wishes. The same groups who expected to retire before age fifty-five are now realizing that they may end up working longer than previously expected. According to a 2003 survey, 72 percent of current workers expect to work part-time long after retirement age while 20 percent expect to work full time. This is a major shift in attitude.

The percentage of people who plan to work during retirement varies from one generation to the next. Sixty-seven percent of preboomers, 69 percent of early boomers, 72 percent of late boomers, and 79 percent of Generation X expect to keep working long after age sixty-five. The reasons cited are obvious: (1) inadequate savings or investments,

(2) inability to plan well, and (3) lack of personal discipline to stay on course with a financial plan.

Youthfulness has many attributes, among which is the ability to dream. But it also carries its share of juvenility. For instance, the ability to talk big, having all knowledge, and taking things lightly are some of the prominent characteristics of youth. In other words, it's one thing to dream about early retirement, but creating the environment to make it happen takes maturity. This is where boys are separated from men, an issue that has very little to do with age.

Supposedly, most workers are adults having the ability to reason, enabling them to peel away nonsense from what's real. Therefore, it's incumbent on each worker to take the retirement issue seriously. Those who do will make the time and effort to be ready. Then they'll reap the benefits of their work when they reach retirement age. But those who continue to squander their precious resources on the present with little regard for the future will be highly disappointed.

CHAPTER 4

A Snapshot of the Emotional State of Most Americans

Given all that we know, money is the most essential economic component in the universe. It provides the means by which we shape our lives through financial choices. We use it to pay for indispensable items such as food, shelter, safety, comfort, and so on. In addition, we use it as a tool to acquire intangible benefits such as freedom, control, and power. For some of us, these attributes have more value than anything else money can buy.

In the American culture, an inadequate amount of money severely limits our choices in life. The less money we have, the less we can do or say. We end up with little no negotiating power, and the quality of goods and services we buy diminishes measurably. For instance, those of us who have the habit of stretching the dollar have no choice but to buy lower-grade merchandise. The same is true for services. Many times, we do the work ourselves or end up compromising with cheap labor.

Additionally, when our financial position is weak, we become more vulnerable to all sort of other issues. We remain threatened by economic changes, e.g., higher prices, higher interest rates, inflation, etc.; we become more sensitive to attacks by creditors; and we become more concerned about the possibility of losing our incomes. At the very least, the absence of money leaves us feeling uneasy and worried.

Some who are financially comfortable and haven't experienced the scarcity of money are undeniably "blessed." At the same time, it becomes easy for them to trivialize the value of money and undermine the serious needs of those who don't have enough. It is not unusual, for example, to hear the following comments from those who feel financially secure: "It's only money, for heaven's sake" or "I don't need money to make me happy."

In some ways, these statements are partly true. Money doesn't necessarily excite anyone, per se. Therefore, it's easy for someone who has never experienced financial hardship to remain insensitive about the needs of those who struggle to make ends meet.

But those who understand the real value of money, take a totally different view. They respect the dollar, not only in terms of its capacity to create happiness but, also, in terms of worth—the things money can buy. Therefore, even though money itself brings no happiness, the things it provides do cultivate happiness.

The evidence of this can be seen when one has little or no money. The concern and constant worry about the commodity are heightened to extreme levels, causing justifiable sadness and discomfort. For instance, there is nothing funny about watching your children suffer with hunger, going without medical and dental insurance, and missing out on the fun things of life just because you can't afford them. Furthermore, there is something to be said about the following situations:

- The rent comes due, and you can't pay it.
- The only car you have needs repair, and you have no funds to fix it.
- A family member dies, and you have no money for the burial.
- You need gas in your car, and the only money you have is the nickel in your pocket.
- You're hungry but can't buy a burger.
- Your refrigerator is empty, but you can't buy groceries to feed your family.
- Creditors are calling you night and day because of delinquent accounts.
- Your house is taken from you and given to someone else because you couldn't pay the mortgage.
- The bank is threatening to take your car next month unless you bring your account up to date.

No, money may not necessarily bring a person happiness, but it certainly calms the nerves under these circumstances. Moreover, it's not hard to imagine that if the things you've come to rely on for comfort and safety are taken away from you, how different life would be.

If you, personally, haven't experienced any of these financial hardships, consider yourself fortunate. You've obviously done a few things right with your finances, and as a result, you're enjoying the fruits of your labor. It could also mean that you may have inherited enough wealth to put you at ease for the rest of your life.

But just because you're financial stable, and can't relate to financial scarcity, don't assume that these situations don't exist in the lives of others. Right here, in the good old United States of America, we're experiencing more personal financial crises than many people realize. Our poor money management skills and big appetite for tantalizing products keep us struggling with our finances each month, a situation millions of us would like to bring under control.

But who could tell that the majority of us are broke? Only a handful of people such as debt management company, banks, financial counselors and planners, mortgage brokers, and so on can tell. The truth is, we've learned to hide the problem well while making others believe that everything is under control.

But as much as we try to keep a lid on the issue, the truth about our finances eventually surfaces. In addition to admitting to someone that we need help, the problem reveals itself through our attitude. We exhibit a general sense of frustration, impatience, and disappointment about life in general. We see it in the home, on the freeway, on the job, in the malls, in the supermarkets, in schools, and even in our churches.

Comprehensively Stretched

Like many Americans, I went to night and weekend classes in order to obtain a college degree. The school I attended was designed primarily for working adults who couldn't attend day classes in a traditional university because of work schedules. Each curriculum course was separated into six-week segments to accelerate the pace and obtain the degree sooner.

While in school, I had an acute observation that will stay with me forever. I saw exhausted people who were intently focused in doing whatever it took to get a college degree in order to either maintain or improve their lifestyles.

The issue wasn't necessarily the rigid determination to accomplish the task, although that was quite obvious. What was unusual was the purpose for which people were attending classes. Though it's true that job seekers need a college degree in order to compete in today's job market, it was the panic-stricken pressure to get that degree that caught my attention. Most of my fellow students were being forced through a process that they would rather do without. Some were in school because they were afraid of losing their jobs to someone else with a college degree. Some had been fired and desperately needed a degree in order to find another job. Yet others had gotten clues of tentative layoffs due to downsizing, and they were preparing themselves for the next job opportunity.

For these individuals, obtaining a college degree was more than social cosmetics. It was a matter of life and death. That degree meant the difference between stable income and being out of a job. As a result, getting it became the main thing in their lives, at least for the time being.

Despite the motive, the process of obtaining that degree didn't come easy. For some students, school was a bygone exercise, and the art of studying had to be renewed. For them, the experience was downright agonizing. Additionally, everyone complained about being tired and overworked. "Not enough time in the day to do everything," was a common phrase around campus. Others talked about the lack of sleep and exercise. Even so, they kept coming to classes regularly.

For me, the whole experience was an inspiration. Not only did I enjoy being in school, but I was also fortunate to have been associated with others who were determined to achieve a specific goal. That attitude excited me.

On the other hand, I often wondered about my fellow students' overall quality of life. Many of them were married with children and had the responsibility of a household. This alone is more than some people can handle. Yet most of these students held fulltime jobs, something that we have come to expect in this culture. Adding to all of these were the normal school requirements such as classroom time and homework assignments.

Few people can accomplish all these responsibilities at the same time and remain sane. This type of routine generally leads to undue stress which creates other physical and emotional issues such as burnout.

In spite of the pressure, however, these people kept attending classes, hoping to graduate. The truth is, their livelihood depended on it, and they felt compelled to be in school.

Call it the spirit of the age, the end time, the American way, or the twenty-first century, the fact is, most Americans feel that life is continually demanding more and more from them each day. It is as though we're forced to do things for two life-times—the one we live, and the one we anticipate to live. Consequently, we feel pulled in many directions.

Meanwhile, we question our priorities: are we doing the right thing, the right way, at the right time, for the right purpose? As we try to answer these questions, we struggle to maintain control over all the demands that are placed on us each day. At the same time, we feel *comprehensively stretched* to our human capacity, wondering how much more can we take.

Excessively Stressed

There is a price for everything, and the cost is not always in dollars and cents. In business, costs generally relate to money and while some are immediate, such as an initial investment to get a company off the ground, others such as payment to a supplier are sometimes delayed 30 to 90 days later. In any case, all costs come due eventually.

In our world of multitasking, the costs of doing business are both immediate and long-term. On a short-term basis, our bodies and minds take a real beating as we go through life doing three or four things at once. We generally drive ourselves to the ground until we become physically spent or motionally exhausted. When that happens, most of us put off fun and recreational activities because we're too tired to do anything else.

As we continue this hectic lifestyle, we eventually create all sorts of other long-term complications. Three of the most prominent ailments of our time are stress, anxiety, and depression. Forty-five million Americans suffer with symptoms of these maladies. In any given year, approximately 21 million adults, age eighteen and older, experience some type of depressive disorder while another 19.1 million people ages eighteen to fifty-four suffer with anxiety.

People who experience depression or anxiety are not necessarily crazy or mentally unstable. They're generally healthy individuals who take life seriously and have too much going on simultaneously. Many of them are high achievers who are trying to make a positive difference in their lives and that of others. But while some of them are able to manage the pressures of life somewhat successfully, others cannot. Emotionally, they succumb to the forces that are brought down upon them, causing internal turmoil. A recent study showed that people with generalized anxiety disorder (GAD) usually expect the worst. They worry excessively about money, health, family, and work issues. As a result, some GAD victims turn to abusive substances such as alcohol and drugs, which ultimately lead to other problems.

Most experts agree that GAD is hereditary. Nonetheless, no one can positively say what causes it. There is evidence suggesting that the condition is aggravated by stress, which is a mental or emotional disruptive state of mind. For most people, however, stress is self-induced from concerns for things such as money, health, family, or work.

This makes sense when you consider that although money, health, family, and work are separate issues, they're interrelated. Therefore, it's not unusual to experience a problem in one area and feel the pain in another. Money, for instance, is always needed to pay for family needs such as medical and dental services, food, shelter, transportation, and more. When these needs are not adequately met as a result of money shortages, negative things happen. Family relationships become weaker, job performance drops, emotional instability rises, financial security becomes unstable, and the level of stress rises.

In the midst of this conflict, we sometimes become irrational. In our desperate need for money, we look for it from various means. Some of us worry about it, hoping it will magically appear. Others work two and three jobs to get enough spending money. Some pray for it, hoping it will rain down from heaven. Some scheme to get it, and others even steal and kill for it.

Each year, millions of us tolerate undue pressure on the job simply because we need the money. A recent poll indicated that more than half of depression sufferers (58 percent) kept their emotional conditions private. When asked why, 45 percent admitted that they didn't want to be labeled as being weak, unstable, or overly emotional. Twenty-five percent feared being fired, and 20 percent didn't want to be overlooked for a promotion.

Job-related stress is one of our biggest issues as a culture. In the adult world, it crosses gender, race, age, education levels, and more. Seven in ten (70 percent) of depressed employees claimed that work pressure contributed directly to their mental and emotional illnesses. Forty percent cited excessive workload, 32 percent referred to bad working environment, 23 percent blamed bullying and harassment on the job, and 21 percent cited long working hours. A 1988 poll indicated that 22 percent of workers were frequently worried about losing their jobs. Another study showed that 40 percent of worker turnover was directly related to job stress.

Today, the endemic nature of this problem is gaining international attention. The United States National Institute for Occupational Safety and Health has reported that job-related stress is fast becoming the most widespread reason for worker disability. In 1992, the United Nations (UN) referred to job stress as "the twentieth-century epidemic," and the World Health Organization called it a "worldwide epidemic."

The cost associated with treating job-related stress, though somewhat invisible, is not cheap. One report estimated that American industries spend between $200 and $300 billion annually. Most of that cost is related directly to absenteeism, employee turnover, diminished productivity, accidents, legal and medical insurance, and workers compensation claims. These costs eventually get passed down to the community in the form of higher prices on goods and services.

Unfortunately, job-related stress isn't easily solved. The issue is more difficult than simply walking away from the work environment. Our livelihood—the money we make, the benefits we receive, the way we dress, the food we eat, etc., depends on it. For most of us, quitting our jobs as a result of job stress is not an option. Doing so also means cutting away our lifelines, provoking even more stress as a result of lack of income.

Therefore, most of us think twice before walking away from the job. The main reason is because the financial ramification is much greater than tolerating the job stress itself. As a result, we endure the pressure for the money. Meanwhile, most of us remain *excessively stressed* as we deal with the day-to-day ordeal. The hope is that things may change for the better—the supervisor may quit his job, or we may end up finding another place to work.

Sharply Stung

As much as we brag about our successes, one would think that we're generally satisfied with our individual progress. But millions of us are highly disappointed about what we haven't accomplished. This is especially true for those who've spent years preparing for their dreams. Each year, they look forward to having more money, greater opportunities, and added success. Yet few of them achieve those desires. Instead, they watch the years roll by with no extra progress.

Still deep down, each of us wants to be special. We want to make some type of contribution to humanity and get recognized for it. We want our names written in books, seen in movies, plastered on buildings, placed in libraries or museums, and talked about in schools.

Some of us have accomplished these things. History is paved with evidence of American greatness. We have huge bridges, incredible monuments, massive highways and skyscrapers, and much more. We've also advanced in areas such as medicine, agriculture, and technology, particularly in communication. Behind each of these achievements, you'll find one or two Americans who were willing to risk their resources to see these things come to fruition.

The reality is, all of us have the physical and mental capacity to do something similar or greater. Unfortunately, few of us take steps to make them happen. Instead, we become complacent with mediocre achievements.

As we age, this reality becomes more evident. Then we're *stung* by the fact that we haven't accomplished our dreams. At the same time, it occurs to us that time is slipping away, leaving us with less of it to waste. Ultimately, most of us are left wishing that we had contributed more to humanity and that we had gotten the respect and recognition we wanted.

Blatantly Stripped

One of the great things about America is the freedom we have to be ourselves. The fact that we're able to attend college, select a career, make all the money we want, buy real estate, and travel tells a lot about this great country. It is certainly a land filled with milk and honey, one in which people can achieve anything their hearts desire.

But in spite of all its bountiful blessings, America makes no promises to anyone. The treasures she provides must be earned. She sets a value on everything and challenges each one of us to pay the price. In the end, much of what we get is determined by our individual commitment and sacrifice.

From the beginning, all lanes of opportunities are wide open for the choosing. Career choices are almost limitless. We have an array of vocational choices, making it easy for anyone to find exactly what he or she wants to do. Some choose the military as a route to the top, some make state and federal jobs their career option, some choose the corporate path to success, some go into business for themselves. Some do nothing at all.

Whichever path we take to get what we want, our ulterior motive is basically the same. We want to succeed in life and make it big. So we choose a career path that promises the greatest benefits, at least that's the way we see it initially.

What we fail to realize is that though we desire to achieve roughly the same results, all career paths don't provide the same outcome. Each one requires knowledge, commitment, and sacrifice, some more than others. By the same token, each produces its specific set of benefits. In other words, one who embarks on a lifetime journey of being a taxi driver will reap a different set of personal, professional, and financial rewards than a personal who chooses to be a computer engineer.

Unfortunately, this situation makes sense to some people only at the end of the journey. When they stop and evaluate what they have accomplished, they're generally surprised to see that some people have attained much more than others. Moreover, the costs of doing business—the physical, emotional, and financial output—generally outweigh the benefits.

I'm reminded of a situation regarding one of my university instructors. She, a doctorate-degree instructor, came to class late consistently. Most of the time, she appeared to be overworked, stressed, and distracted. As soon as she walked into the classroom, she would breathlessly apologize for being late and blamed the traffic for her tardiness. Then more often than not, she made comments about her personal issues and her hectic lifestyle.

After three weeks of listening to a modified version of her personal life, I finally said to her, "Jane [not her real name], I'm confused.

I'm here to get a college degree, hoping to *improve* my personal circumstances. To this point, it is my understanding that the more education one has, the easier life becomes, e.g., a better career, more money, more options, more free time, less stress, and so on. But frankly, your situation, as a PhD graduate, seems to indicate something entirely different. In fact, it appears that your life is extremely busy and stressful, contrary to what I expected."

She apologized for her demeanor. Then she said, "You're right. My job is very stressful, and I'm doing my best with the situation. The sad thing about it is I need this teaching job to pay for the huge student loan I accumulated during my education."

I empathized with her situation, hoping never to put myself in this type of predicament. Since then, however, I've come to realize that she isn't the only one who is trapped in this quagmire. Millions of us have taken steps to achieve our dreams, and the process has drained our energy and enthusiasm. In the end, we walk away feeling *stripped*—a feeling of being battered, spent, and exhausted.

The worst feeling of all is that many of us have come to the end of the road and have nothing to show in exchange for the struggle. Our hard work has been costly, both in terms of money and personal sacrifice. Yet the benefits have been negligible. In many ways, we're worse off than we were when we got started. In regards to money, the majority of us are not only broke, but we're also deep in debt, a financial burden that lingers for years. As a result, many of us feel misled, cheated, and unfulfilled. It's as though our confidence, self-esteem, and dignity have been *stripped* away, leaving us confused and vulnerable.

Indecisively Stuck

"Where do we go from here?" is not a comforting question. Since so many of us feel exhausted, the answer remains vague. Daily, we're reassessing our remaining resources—time, money, and energy—trying to decide what to do next. The truth is, after years of beating the pavement and getting nowhere, we're reluctant to try something new. In short, we're *indecisively stuck.*

Psychologically, some people have confessed feeling as though they're trapped in a muddy hole. And the harder they try to pull themselves out of the pit, the deeper they fall. This type of experience is usually a direct response to some type of physical or emotional trauma such a divorce, bankruptcy, or near-death experience. Those who are determined to go on usually survive the ordeal. At the same time, they generally walk away with indelible scars as a reminder.

Some people believe that it's never too late to do something worthwhile: attaining a college degree, setting up a business, and so on. Personally, I support that philosophy. But realistically, some of us have missed opportunities that may never come around again. Furthermore, life has a way of trying to crush people who are unprepared to do whatever is necessary to survive. And after being buffeted around too many times, they give up hope of winning by refusing to tolerate any more abuse.

This explains the prevailing attitude of some workers. According to financial experts, Americans need additional motivation beyond what's currently available in order to improve their financial condition. Since current means (the college degree, the good job, and the high salaries) have failed to provide them financial success, gathering the extra effort to continue is nothing more than futility. For instance, an additional job doesn't necessarily mean more money for the family. Instead, people visualize an arrangement for the government to gain more taxes which leaves them with less money to spend.

This deflated attitude is not isolated to one segment of the population. It crosses all ages, gender, and socio-economic status. This type of situation proves that people can tolerate only so much disappointment before they surrender completely. And when that happens, what was once important suddenly becomes insignificant.

But admitting defeat is not necessarily the solution, either. Whenever one capitulates under pressure, the person relinquishes control to the adversary (in this case, the economy) who then takes the upper hand in the fight. At that point, the future becomes unpredictable, leaving the person feeling somewhat hopeless and *stuck.*

It's not hard to distinguish people who are stuck and have given up on life. They have no dreams or purpose, and they wonder around aimlessly. As a result, the years come and go, leaving them no better off than the year before. And although they feel useless and unproductive, they have no idea how to change their circumstances. So, they "settle for" whatever comes their way—a day by day existence where one feels unprepared for what's ahead.

Indefinitely Stopped

In the game of chess, as long as the opponent is willing to play, there is a chance for a weak player to win a game or two. For that to happen, though, the person must be willing to learn a new strategy in order to beat the challenger. Otherwise, he or she will keep losing the game and eventually get discouraged. When this happens, no harm is done except for a bruised ego, which has the capacity to heal quickly.

We can't say the same in the game of finance. Mistakes are less forgiving and more permanent. For instance, after spending all your money, if you resort to borrowing additional funds for more shopping, you're likely to keep loosing the financial game. On a long-term basis, you've jeopardized your financial security, something that's not always easily fixed overnight. And on a short-term basis, you will experience other problems such as the inability to pay off debts, character damage, and lack of savings.

Those of us who have fallen prey to debt remember the sting of the monster. Some of us have scars that will last forever as a result of the bite. Yet circumstances and personal habits keep us going back into the jungle to be bitten again and again. It is as though when we have escaped the jaws of the beast with minor scratches, we feel compelled to go back until it puts us flat on our backs. Most of us feel that we need to borrow money to live our lives. And it is this type of thinking that keeps us broke and economically disadvantaged. And until we change our thinking, the habit will continue until we're hurt too badly to care.

The math is simple: the *more debt* we carry, the *longer the term;* the *more interest* we pay, the *more broke* we become.

After years of borrowing, we eventually see the light. Suddenly, it becomes apparent that we're simply existing to be bills and debts. Faced with this dilemma, we feel hopelessly trapped in a cycle of regressive productivity. We're accomplishing little or nothing at all as we age.

Yet, the reality of being caught in a web of debt is not something that can be dismissed quickly. All of us can attest to the fact that while debt can be created in weeks or months, it takes years to undo the damage. Meanwhile, the pressure of holding everything together with our limited resources becomes overbearing.

Long-term, our minds and bodies begin to react to the strain in predictable ways, e.g., fear, tension, stress, anxiety, depression, and other physiological complications. Ultimately, everything climaxes to a condition I refer to as *financially checkmate,* a stalemate or immobilized position triggered by lack of financial success or control.

When we get to this point, we *stop indefinitely.* And the only way to move forward is to start the game over, hopefully with renewed motivation and financial insight.

No Need for Science

The desire to survive is one of the greatest motivations in the universe. In fact, the energy can be so strong that it takes us to the brink of insanity. For instance, human beings can become so desperately hungry that they become irrational and start devouring one another for lunch. It has happened at sea and under other difficult conditions. The same is true for every other living species.

In a civil arrangement, our survival instincts are more civilized. We learn to practice what's common to the masses while reserving our most irrational behavior for desperate moments as we try to build a life for ourselves.

The assessment in this chapter is unscientific, as you can tell. In fact, the entire narrative is based purely on observation and statistical data. We need no scientific validation in this situation. Our personal experiences (yours, mine, those of my clients, and millions of other Americans) provide enough proof. In fact, nothing is more accurate to you than your own personal circumstances. So you become the judge and the jury.

How did we get here? What's causing our financial failure? And more importantly, what can be done to prevent or undo this life-choking experience?

Here is the typical American path to financial prosperity: During the journey, you'll probably recognize where you may have gone wrong— mistakes or bad judgments you made—which ultimately prevented you from attaining the financial independence you hoped to achieve.

CHAPTER 5

A Cultural Path to a Predictable Outcome

Whenever I get the opportunity to present a financial workshop or training to a younger group, I generally approach the audience by asking them the following question, "By a show of hands, how many of you would like to be financially successful?" Almost every time, I get 100 percent response, except two or three people who would be either too embarrassed to raise their hands or simply don't want to admit the truth.

The response to the next question is just as fascinating. "When is the best time to start making financial preparation for retirement?"

"Yesterday," some would say. "Now," others would echo in a different part of the room. "As soon as possible," a few others would reply.

Theoretically, all the answers are correct. Retirement planning should be started as early as possible. And based on the response from the audience, the majority of them believe that to be true. In practice, however, few of them make use of what they believe because when I ask the same group, "Why haven't the majority of you started preparing?" they remain quiet. In other words, they know that retirement planning should be done early, but doing it becomes a challenge. The truth of the matter is, most of them don't know how to begin preparing for retirement or don't have the money to get the process started.

But can we blame young Americans for not practicing what they know to be right in regards to money and finance? No. The reality is, the culture is partly responsible for their attitude and behavior. Since it encourages young Americans to wait until their mid-twenties to take life seriously, retirement planning is also delayed at least that long. Until then, American youths treat life as an experimental game as they wait for everything to be done for them. Meanwhile, retirement planning gets pushed ahead to their thirties and forties when they think that they'll have lots of time and money to handle the annoying issue.

What they don't realize is that there is no better time to address the subject than in the late teens and early twenties. While it's true that the initial steps can be started at any time prior to the late teens, the six-year period between eighteen and twenty-four years old is crucial to establishing a strong financial base. Missing this opportunity makes retirement planning more difficult in the years ahead.

That is not to say a person cannot become wealthy after age twenty-four. Such a thought would be preposterous. Anyone can become financially successful at any age, an event that happens almost every day in this country. However, if an individual wants to become wealthy by using the principle of compounding interest, the sooner the person gets started, the more successful he or she becomes.

Getting young Americans to understand and apply the concept of compounding interest is not easy, though. Their logic is, any money invested too early is money that can't be enjoyed today.

Walking Away from the Nest (Young Adults)

For most young Americans, life begins at eighteen years old. Having been pushed, pulled, dictated to, and controlled by parents, teachers, and relatives, they feel liberated as they walk away from home into adulthood. This is the moment they dreamed about for years: stepping into a world of fun and adventure with no rules or restrictions. There, they'll indulge themselves with all kinds of activities that appease their six senses. For most of them, that includes late-night parties, sex, alcohol, drugs, fast foods, beach parties, drag racing, and a whole lot more.

Granted, these recreational activities are not isolated to young people. Culturally, we all participate in them to one degree or another. However, the pleasure-seeking nature of young adults is more conducive to these types of activities; therefore, they're more apt to be drawn to them.

The accompanying attitude to this type of lifestyle is just as intriguing. Although they have no idea where they came from, they adopt an overly confident approach on life, thinking that they're invincible. Thus, life is eternal. Accordingly, they challenge death itself as they explore their world looking for thrills.

Parallel to this mindset is an incredible ability to show their ignorance without flinching. Since they generally know the answer to everything, no recommendation is good enough. Their parents are simply boneheads who lack common sense, and everyone else is out of touch with reality.

Meanwhile, they deliberately avoid taking anything too seriously. Their job, for instance, is no big deal. Although it provides them a paycheck, they have no desire to be loyal, prompt, or dependable. Furthermore, since they remain uncommitted to the job, they're ready to walk away at anytime, ready to prove their independence.

Yet they plan to acquire a lot of wealth—the best of everything. Somehow, they believe that possessions are easy to get, and in time, these things will magically come together without any struggle. As a result, they feel no rush to get things done, including financial planning. For them, there is lots of time to take care of this matter.

Then, they come to grips with reality. It occurs to them that nothing in life is free. And if they want to succeed financially, the onus rests squarely on their shoulders.

They also realize that being an adult is not as much fun as they once imagined. This new revelation requires a totally different approach to life if one has to succeed. It entails having the courage to handle responsibilities and the backbone to accept consequences for personal behavior.

Armed with this new perspective, life takes on a different form. The value of *money* suddenly becomes more important. They realize that in addition to using dollars and cents to pay for basic necessities and more, *money* has the capacity to endow one with control, power, and recognition, attributes most people privately desire.

Somewhere during this new finding, they also learn that the process of accumulating money is not easy. It necessitates some type of trade-off, particularly physical or mental work, forcing them into a position to make a career choice. Faced with the following four possibilities, namely, (1) going to college, (2) joining the military, (3) enrolling in a trade school, or (4) jumping directly into the workforce, they make a decision.

Regardless which career path they take, the outcome is basically the same. The ulterior motive is *money*. And as far as they're concerned, the more the better. They stay focused on creating the dollar because without it, nothing gets done.

In time, they join the work force. But within all the dynamics of life—holding a job, making money, and having fun—they run into another surprising challenge: a money-management dilemma. Seemingly, every dollar they make gets spent. Worse, the more they make, the more they spend, creating an ongoing need for additional money. In the midst of this confusion, retirement planning becomes less of a priority with each paycheck. And once again, the idea gets pushed further into the future.

By this time, they're between twenty and twenty-four years old. They have been aging but haven't realized it. And each day they put off saving and investing money, they're actually getting closer to the poorhouse, a reality they'll live to regret.

The Life Cycle Expectation Timeline

According to the *Life Cycle Expectation Timeline* (an unofficial index designed to track our financial progress with time), in order to stay current with time or aging, between eighteen and twenty-four years old, our *net worth* should be close to $25,000 (see figure 5.1).

Timeline
(Years of your life)

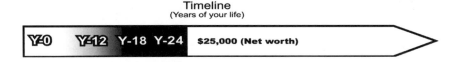

Fig. 5.1

A portion of this wealth should be invested in some type of cash or liquid assets, of which seventy-five to 80 percent should be marked for capital growth investments and roughly 20 percent contributed to an income fund.

Additionally, if we don't own a house, we should be looking for one. Whether we decide to buy or rent, there should be money set aside for furniture. Moreover, we should have our own transportation instead of having to rely on others—private or public.

When it comes to retirement planning, no time is more appropriate than the early twenties. This is the period to buckle down and start contributing a fixed amount of our income to savings.

Your Reality

What do you say? Do you have $25,000 net worth? If you don't, I'm not surprised. The eighteen to twenty-four year olds in my audience didn't have it, either. And as far as they were concerned, whoever came up with this measurement is out of touch with reality because no one they knew had this kind of net worth.

But when you stop and think about it, a $25,000 net worth between the ages of twenty and twenty-four years old is not an impossible feat. First, it's said that American children between the ages of four and twelve years old generate $17 billion annually. Trained properly, some of this money could be put to good use. Second, a net worth of any amount doesn't necessarily suggest a sum of cash but rather a combination of hard and liquid assets. Third, we must assume that a few twenty year olds do have a net worth in excess of $25,000—cash or assets they've accumulated themselves. Therefore, it is possible for young Americans to accumulate a sizeable sum of money by the time they're twenty-four years old. Most of them make enough to do it.

Settling Down

Emerging from, seemingly, a confused phase in life, this is the time most twenty-four or twenty-five year olds begin to take life seriously. It is as though they wake up one day and realize that life is leaving them behind. Consequently, they do everything they can to catch up. Those who see corporate America as a way to financial independence make a mad dash to find their place in the system. Others follow their passion for success in other areas of interest. This is the time they also contemplate getting married, raising a family, and starting an investment regimen.

For Your Benefit

Assume that you're one of the twenty-five year old Americans we've been describing. You're, in fact, getting ready to put your life together just like the others. You think you know how to bring all the pieces of your life together in order to be successful. You may have a college degree, and you're banking on it as your salvation. In fact, you've been told that without the degree, you can't be successful. Therefore, you're hanging your hopes on it and wishing for the best.

You're going to be tested. In fact, many of your trials will be unavoidable unless you know what they are and have prepared yourself for the challenges ahead. But that's unlikely because we generally don't know what the future holds.

So let's fast-forward your life, step by step, to retirement age. The scenarios will be brief and simple, but the message will be clear. It will give you insight in the life of the average American who walks through the economic pathway in this country. You will see the mistakes people make and learn to avoid them, thereby, improving your personal circumstances for the rest of your life.

Getting Hitched

You're approximately twenty-five years old, definitely single, and on your own. You have a job that provides decent wages, and you want to be financially well-off by the time you retire. For the time being, your life is as simple as it will ever be. If you're renting a small apartment, chances are, you're sleeping on a couch or sofa—if you have one, eating fast foods for most of your meals, spending your entire paycheck on yourself, and making minimum payments on your credit cards.

You like your situation. But you don't intend to live this way for the rest of your life. You plan to get married someday but have no idea when that will be. Like most of your contemporaries, you want to wait for the right moment because you realize that getting married is a big step. More than the cost of the wedding and reception, maintaining a home is a huge financial responsibility. Therefore, you feel it's prudent to wait until you're financially able to support a family.

This is a sensible decision. But unfortunately, you will be coerced into getting married long before you're ready. One of the main reasons for the hurry is that most parents can't wait to have grandchildren. The situation provides them the opportunity to once again live through their grandchildren. Therefore, in spite of your efforts to delay the event, you will give in to the pressure.

Then, what you feared the most will have come to pass. You're now married and have complicated your life, seemingly, overnight. If you're the only person in the family who brings in a paycheck, you're about to experience a financial fiasco: The one-bedroom apartment has suddenly gotten too small for you, your spouse, and prospective children. So, you're ready to go hunting for a bigger place to live.

In addition to the bigger apartment, you'll end up purchasing many more items. Over the course of several months, you'll buy furniture, entertainment systems, kitchenware, and a host of other things to make the house comfortable. The said truth is, most of these items will be purchased on credit.

Shortly after the purchasing spree, you're starting to experience a cash-flow problem. By the time you pay the higher rent, more food, utilities, transportation, credit card payments, and so on, you have little or no money left for other things. Your paycheck suddenly vanishes right before your eyes.

Then comes another unexpected situation. Roughly six months after the wedding, your parents will start looking for signs of pregnancy. They want grandchildren. And should you hesitate to perform your duty, they'll insist that you get your act together.

At first, you wanted to delay getting married because you were not financially ready to undertake the responsibility. But now that you're married, the pressure to have children has also dominated your attention, so much so that you no longer fight the issue. You want children. So you take the necessary steps to have them.

But your decision to have children doesn't change the facts about raising them. The cost, particularly, is extremely high. According to the U.S. Department of Agriculture, by the time a child who was born in 2000 reached six years old, parents with an annual income of $64,000 or more will have spent $97,762 providing for the child. That's approximately $16,000 a year in expenses for one child.

Keep in mind that this is only the beginning. As you can tell, these figures do not reflect the cost of raising the child until eighteen years old. Moreover, if you intend to pay for college, you'll be faced with an average price of $40,000 a year, a sum few parents can afford to pay these days. And for those with more than one child, the costs are exorbitant.

This is one of the main reasons some people rethink the child issue. They simply can't imagine spending that much money to raise one child. As a result, they postpone pregnancy until they are financially able to provide adequately for children. Others limit their offspring to one or two children. Yet some disregard the cost altogether while focusing on their personal desire to have children. It's as though they're led to believe that emotional concerns—love alone, for example—will keep the children fed, clothed, sheltered, and educated. Unfortunately, in these types of situations, the real truth comes too late. And the children are the ones who suffer most.

The point is not that people shouldn't get married and have children, but that they must become aware of the financial implications regarding the decision. If financial independence is someone's goal, raising a family concurrently makes the task much more difficult or, in most cases, nearly impossible.

Notwithstanding, the choice to have children ultimately comes down to individual families. For instances, there are people who feel that they must have children, and they take the liberty to do so. There are those who experience difficulty in having children and are willing to do everything in their power to discover the satisfaction of pregnancy. Yet there are some who want nothing to do with the inconvenience of pregnancy, the pain of childbirth, and the cost of rearing children. All options are perfectly okay in our culture.

On the other hand, *not* all those who plan to have children are automatically resigned to a life of poverty. On the contrary, some people use their family (spouse and children) as a reason to be financially successful. For those individuals, the equation provides a magical combination for extra motivation. They simply get "fired up" or passionately determined to create better living conditions for their family. This is not the case with most people, because this type of attitude requires additional sacrifices.

Those who choose to remain single and childless have no guarantee of financial success, either. We all know that a single person could have a large income and yet remain broke throughout life. The reality is that all of us have a tendency to spend our money on a variety of activities germane to our interests. Unfortunately, some people (married or single) make irrational financial decisions that translate into unreasonable outcomes.

Yet, it's reasonable to assume that those who remain single and childless have more money at their disposal. Since their priorities are laid out differently, they have a better chance of taking advantage of economic opportunities. It's up to them to channel their financial resources sensibly.

In contrast, those who get married and decide to raise children have a bigger financial challenge. The extra expense for things such as clothes, shoes, food, medical and dental care can quickly deplete a budget. Eighteen years of this type of spending, multiplied by the number of children, will keep most families broke.

It is in this condition we find you roughly five years after being married. Since your financial responsibilities have increased as a result of having children, you've come to rely more and more on credit cards to make ends meet. Today, you have difficulty staying afloat each month, and you're wondering what happened. You are, what you've come to understand to be, *financially checkmate.*

You're now in your early thirties and broke. Meanwhile, the clock has been ticking, and you are aging.

The Life Cycle Expectation Timeline

Here is the expected financial progress in regard to your age. According to experts, if you're between twenty-five to thirty-four years old (see figure 5.2), you should have an average net worth of $50,000.

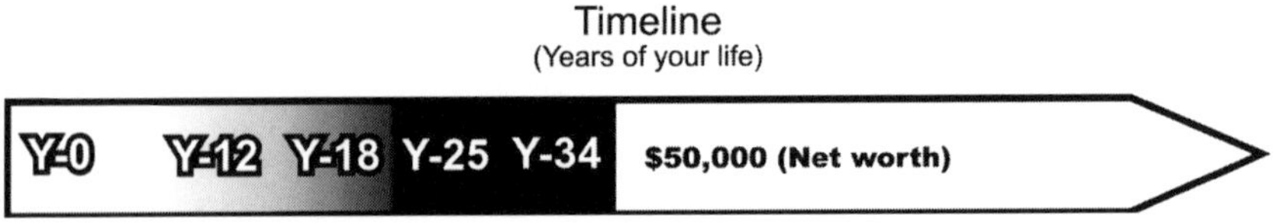

Timeline
(Years of your life)

| Y-0 | Y-12 | Y-18 | Y-25 | Y-34 | $50,000 (Net worth) |

Fig. 5.2

You should be contributing no less than 7 percent of your gross income into a retirement fund, 65 to 75 percent of which should be placed in a growth fund while approximately 30 percent allocated to an income and safety fund.

Expenses are expected to increase in key areas such as housing and child rearing during this period. Therefore, you should be keenly aware of credit card usage in order to prevent runaway spending.

When you get a promotion, you should consider increasing your savings and other types of investments, among which should include children's college funds and tax-deferred retirement accounts. Also, since family insurance is usually overlooked, this is a good time to re-evaluate policies to make sure that everyone is adequately covered.

Estate planning is another area of concern. If this process hasn't been implemented, now is a good time to do so. The plan should be drafted by a competent attorney, and it should clearly spell out all ben-eficiaries as well as appropriate guardianship for children.

Well, what do you think? Based on this scenario, have you missed the mark altogether? Since you have increased your debt and haven't saved any money, your net worth is probably zero. It could be that you have a 401(k) retirement plan with moderate growth, but when you do the math, your financial plan is desperately lacking.

A Call for Backup

At this point in your life, you're somewhat perplexed. You feel trapped and don't know how it happened. As you continue searching for answers to your financial dilemma, you recalculate that an extra $500 a month would do the trick. You would have enough money to maintain your debt payments and pay for the extras. So you discuss the situation with your mate, and together, you came up with a solution. Both of you will take jobs to generate extra income and pay off the credit card debts. Your spouse's employment will be temporary. In fact, as soon as the fi-nancial pressure is relieved, the temporary job will end.

There are other issues. The extra employment is going to require additional changes, none of which are going to be easy. With both of you working, you must make arrangements for day care and after school pickups for the children. And since your spouse needs separate trans-portation, you will need to lease or buy another vehicle.

As you're preparing for two jobs, hoping to solve your financial problems, other issues come into focus. With both parents working, life has become more hectic than ever. As the job continues to demand more from you each day, so do the children. In addition to regular school assignments, your children are also involved in extracurricular activities, creating a scheduling nightmare for the family.

To keep up with the demands, both of you must make additional sacrifices. That means you're taking turns to make sure that the children continue their activities. Needless to say, all of this running around eventually takes its toll on you and the rest of the family, leaving everyone exhausted at the end of the day.

You eventually get accustomed to your way of life—you and your spouse are holding full-time jobs while caring for children at the same time. In fact, the whole routine has become very natural because the majority of Americans are doing the same thing. Both parents, in almost every household in this country, hold full-time jobs.

Isn't this the condition in our culture that we refer to as the "rat race"—the process by which we are encouraged to get married before we're financially ready; where both parents are working full-time jobs to make ends meet; and the idea of staying busy all day juggling responsibilities while raising two or more children?

If this is acceptable, why do most of us complain about our condition? The truth is, the majority of us believe that life should be much easier. Yet, few of us know how to change it to our taste. This is your situation.

Although your stress level has mounted as a result of financial pressure and busy lifestyle, no one comes to your rescue. You're in this alone. Even if your friends and relatives would want to alleviate your pain by giving you cash, they can't do it. They too are strapped and find it hard to provide any financial assistance.

The Expansion

Despite the fact that life has become more chaotic for you as a result of your many family obligations, it appears that you're doing well under the circumstances. Somehow, the extra money makes the whole thing more palatable. If for no other reason, you now have more spending power which creates an avenue to vent your frustrations. Consequently, you get distracted from your original goal of paying down your debt and investing some money.

Instead, you're now determined to take advantage of the money while you have it. That means, some of the items that you haven't been able to buy such as the big screen television, the new car, the bedroom set, and so on, have now come into focus. At the same time, you took the opportunity to invest in a home.

Congratulations. You have now expanded your lifestyle by purchasing all the trappings that make up the American dream. And oh, the sensations that come with them. There is nothing more exciting, for example, than walking into a brand-new house that belongs to you. One gets the feeling of success, a rewarding exuberance that says, "I'm finally here." And speak nothing of the smell and comfort of a new car. They add spice and flavor to life every time. So here you are with all your paraphernalia basking in your accomplishments.

Unfortunately, you haven't realized that you've complicated your financial situation. Just about everything you own was bought on credit. And from this time forward, your lifestyle requires two full-time incomes to maintain it. As a result, your spouse's employment, which was intended to be temporary, has now turned into a full-time, "got to have it" second income. Losing it will destroy your economic arrangement and put you on the road to financial ruin.

Meanwhile, within all the fanfare, you've lost track of time and haven't noticed that you, your spouse, and the children are getting older. And, with the aging, comes additional financial burdens. The children now need more clothes, shoes, and other items that require additional funds, creating a bigger financial burden for you. Moreover, the extra debt you created is now beginning to put additional strain on the budget. At this time, you would welcome some additional money on your paycheck, but there is no expectation of a promotion in the near future.

In short, you're experiencing a serious cash-flow problem, again. You're being choked financially but don't know how it happened. The truth is, you need more money to preserve your financial condition, but getting it is another problem. Of course, you can always take a part-time job, but that would add more stress to your current situation. To add insult to injury, your children are getting ready to graduate from high school and making preparation to go to college. Financially, you're not ready to face that responsibility.

At this time, you can follow the popular practice by pulling some equity from the house. But doing so will make things worse. You may be able solve the immediate money crunch, but the problem will still exist. More debt on the house simply creates a bigger financial strain for you in the future.

It's several years later, and you've aged. For some reason, time hasn't stopped to consider your situation. So, you're now in your mid-forties.

The Life Cycle Expectation Timeline

Referring again to the *Life Cycle Expectation Timeline,* between thirty-five and forty-four years old, a person's net worth should be in the vicinity of $150,000 and growing (see figure 5.3).

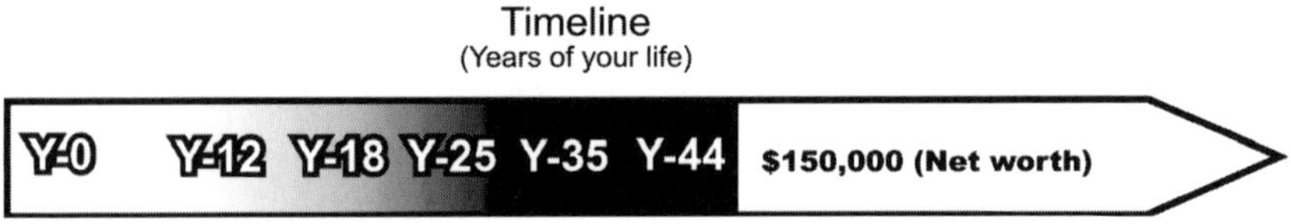

Timeline
(Years of your life)

Y-0   Y-12 Y-18 Y-25 Y-35 Y-44 $150,000 (Net worth)

Fig. 5.3

According to this model, if we start investing at age thirty-five, we should be contributing more than 10 percent of our gross income to a retirement account. Fifty-five to 65 percent of the money should be dedicated to a growth fund while roughly 35 percent allocated to a safety and income fund.

Time should be devoted to reviewing other vital financial components such as insurance policies, children's educational funds, and estate planning.

The Life Cycle Expectation Timeline

Those of us who are between forty-five and fifty-five years old should have a net worth of roughly $300,000 (see figure 5.4).

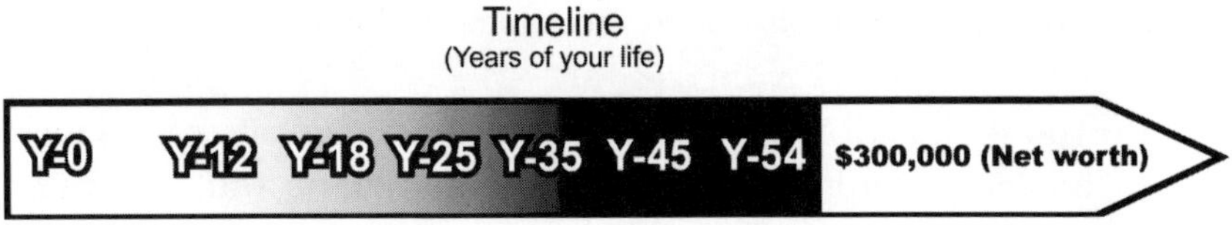

Timeline
(Years of your life)

| Y-0 | Y-12 | Y-18 | Y-25 | Y-35 | Y-45 | Y-54 | $300,000 (Net worth) |

Fig. 5.4

We who are starting to invest at age forty-five should be contributing roughly 18 percent of our gross income into a retirement account. Forty-five to 55 percent of the invested portion should be allocated to a growth fund while roughly 40 percent allocated to an income and safety fund.

The Awakening

Comparing your situation with these models, your net worth is nowhere close to $300,000 or even $150,000 for that matter. You have fallen short of the mark again. Here is why. Your 401(k) plan has grown a little, but you might have taken a portion of it as a down payment for the house. And although your house has appreciated in value, chances are, you've taken some of the equity to pay for children's college education or credit card debt. You think you still have some assets remaining. But when you calculate your net worth, your situation continues to reveal a fragile economic posture.

At this point, it's worth noting that Americans who arrived at their late forties and early fifties with a net worth of $300,000 or more have done well. Of course, this evaluation is based solely on the preceding model. As such, they should be applauded for their efforts because this type of accomplishment requires commitment.

At the same time, most of the wealth is expected to be in cash instruments as opposed to the equity in the home. The truth is, millions of people are banking on the equity in their houses as a major part of their net worth. But that's not entirely reliable because the appreciated value in a residence presents a problem, a questionable situation at best. Consider the following,

1. House equity is based on market value, which is volatile. One day the equity is there, and another day, it's gone,

2. The equity in the house never comes available until the house is sold,

3. Those who sell their houses to retrieve the equity from it remain homeless until they purchase another house with the gains, and

4. When an equity line of credit is taken or the property is refinanced and part of the equity is drawn out, homeowners end up with more debt, which ultimately reduces their net worth.

It's easy to see how some people can stay broke. Even families with a combined income of more than $200,000 a year can end up with a negative net worth. Remember, it's not how much money a person takes home, but what happens to it when it gets there.

Being broke at twenty is one thing, but being broke and in debt at forty is totally different. At twenty, a person can easily say, "Heck, I'm still young, and there's a lot of time ahead to take care of things," a popular view, which is part of the main problem. But at age forty and the mid-fifties, one cannot use these excuses.

In fact, this is the time when most people begin to feel disappointed about life, which is more or less where we find you today. Openly, you appear to be doing well. But privately, you feel unfulfilled and physically exhausted. The reality is that your debt is sapping your energy, and the pressure shows no signs of abating soon. Honestly, this was not where you expected to be at this point in your life: broke, in debt, and physically spent.

But in spite of your financial condition, you take comfort in the fact that few people know about your predicament. You've been hiding it so well. The truth is, unless your economic situation falls apart completely or you don't openly admit the truth to others, few people would guess that you're broke.

From the outside looking in, your financial situation is well masked by your possessions. Your beautiful home, new car, nice clothes, and job title do a wonderful job in hiding your secret. In other words, *you're looking good, smelling good, talking big, but staying broke.* And as long as you're able to maintain your present employment, you'll live like this for years. So to the public, you convey the message that you're financially stable. But privately, your whole financial condition makes you nervous.

But if it's any consolation, you're not the only one in America who experiences this type of problem. The majority of the so-called middle-class people in this country can feel your pain. Millions of us are surviving month by month, paycheck by paycheck, hoping the situation doesn't get worse. In fact, those of who make six digit income are probably no better off than those with less. And in many ways, some are worse off as a result of too much debt.

The Years of Gold

You're now in your late fifties and quickly approaching your retire-ment age. But the golden years you expected to experience don't exist. The color is closer to copper, instead.

The Life Cycle Expectation Timeline

According to the *Life Cycle Expectation Timeline,* between the ages of fifty-five and sixty-four years old, our net worth should be in excess of $400,000 (see figure 5.5).

Timeline
(Years of your life)

Fig. 5.5

By this time, we should be focusing more on capital preservation. For instance, 35 to 45 percent of our investment should be placed in a growth fund while allocating approximately 60 percent in an income and safety fund.

Additionally, we should be looking for options to help minimize investment risks while reducing our tax burden. Other concerns should include long-term health care, specifically in the area of health, life, and disability insurance. Moreover, an umbrella liability-insurance policy should be considered. The aim is to cover any potential threats or risks to our assets.

Also, we should be making preparations to adjust our lifestyle. That includes taking care of issues such as Social Security income and estate planning. And we should be mentally and emotionally prepared to assist aging parents while keeping our own health intact.

Current State of Retirees

Based on the preceding model, few Americans at age sixty-four or sixty-five years old have a net worth of $400,000. In fact, many would say that this marginal net worth is unrealistic. Reemphasizing what's already mentioned in Chapter 3 regarding retirees, a 1996 survey indicated that only 30 percent of them have enough money to live comfortably during retirement.

Medical cost is another major issue that affects older Americans. A whopping 72 percent of people between forty-five and sixty-four years old are having trouble paying their medical bills after treatment. Adding to this problem is the issue of health care insurance. A survey showed that 60 percent of people between fifty-five and sixty-four years old did not get the medical care they needed because of lack of health insurance.

Simply stated, the overall lifestyle of many retired Americans remains questionable. In addition to a day-by-day survival ordeal, they worry about the future of life-sustaining programs such as Social Security and Medicare. Two in five say that their lifestyle is worse now than when they worked. And two in ten say that their lives are a lot worse since they retired. Furthermore, two in five say that retirement is a time of depression—a life plagued with financial problems, poor health, and a feeling of uselessness.

An Assessment

The cultural path to financial prosperity in America is, at best, predictable. For the average American, it's a disappointing one. Most people are poorer by the time they get to retirement age than when they got started.

The following information paints a grim picture. According to the Social Security Administration, 46 percent of current retirees dependent on relatives; 31 percent dependent on charity or welfare; 24 percent are still working to make ends meet; and 2 percent are self-sustaining. Additionally, 86 out of 100 people reaching age 65 do not have $250 in their savings accounts. Ninety-two percent of this group blamed poor planning for their lack of financial success.

How close did the preceding scenarios came to depicting your real situation? If you're in your fifties or older, my guess is that they came very close. On the other hand, if you're in your twenties, only some of them are relatable. But that's the point. As mentioned at the beginning of this chapter, you don't want to experience these problems, if you can help it. The only way to avert them is to start your planning early.

If you find these examples to be somewhat disturbing, I'm not surprised. The truth can be quite painful. The intent here is not to trivialize your financial situation, but to show you that while it's convenient to put off retirement planning, doing so is a major mistake.

"The great law of culture is: Let each becomes all that he was created capable of being; expand, if possible, to his full growth; resisting all impediments, casting off all foreign, especially all noxious adhesions; and show himself at length in his own shape and stature, be these what they may."

THOMAS CARLYLE (1795-1881).

PART II

Causes of the Problem

SEVEN (7) CULTURAL TRAPS DESIGNED TO KEEP YOU BROKE

Now that you've assessed the current and likely financial future of the average American, you're about to embark on a journey into the possible causes of the problem. In the next few chapters, you'll be exposed to some of the most influencing factors in our culture that hinder us from becoming financially successful. Many of them may surprise you because they're so common to our way of life. Yet we don't seem to recognize how they're counterproductive to our financial goals.

Every group has its customs, governing rules or habits, that set it apart from other civilizations. Many of these rules are written into law. Yet others are simply repeated habits adopted from previous generations.

Cultural rules, or laws, are not necessarily designed to create differences between one group of people or another, but to institute lifesaving habits within the culture based on its legends, geography, climatic conditions, available resources, and anticipated changes.

For instance, the manner in which people drive their vehicles, educate their children, and pay their income taxes are likely to be legislative decrees that benefit the masses. On the other hand, the way they eat their dinner and spend their money may be attributed to practices developed through years of repetition. Some groups do not eat food with utensils such as forks, knives, and spoons. They use their fingers instead. And while this habit may appear to be uncouth for one set of people, something like this becomes an identifiable mark for those who practice it.

The customs of a group (however originated) should benefit the members, particularly the individual household. They should cultivate a positive attitude, stimulate the mind, and promote other healthy habits in the weakest of them all.

But unfortunately, all customs are not necessarily healthy and positive. In fact, some are downright punitive, evoking excruciating pain and suffering. One that comes to mind is the *foot-binding* practice in China. For centuries, all women, as early as four years old, had their healthy feet bound in cloth to prevent them from growing longer than three inches (3"). To accomplish this, all the toes, except the big one, were folded under the foot, forcing them to grow in that fashion. Those who were compelled to participate in the ritual complained about the severe pain they endured as they walked. But more than the pain, many of them developed a variety of illnesses, including gangrene.

Needless to say, the women complied with the law because the alternative was just as ruthless. The government made sure that all women shoes were made no larger than three inches. Moreover, women couldn't be married unless their feet were bound as specified by law or custom.

Fortunately, it's been several decades since the *foot-binding* practice has ended. Today, however, there are many older women in China who still carry the evidence of the painful ordeal because their feet will never be normal again.

In regards to the issue of finance, we find both good and bad habits in different cultures. For instance, the Japanese have been known to promote family savings, an idea that supports the individual unit within the group, both short-term and long-term. In the early 1990s, their average savings rate was 15 percent of household income. Today, although the rate has dropped to 5 percent, they're still maintaining the healthy, savings practice.

In contrast, the American culture does the opposite. It focuses on the masses as opposed to the individual family. One way to tell is through our spending and savings habits. In the early 1990s, we saved an average of 7 percent of household income. Today, our savings rate is less than 1percent of after-tax dollars. The bulk of the money we make goes directly back into the market to stimulate the economy. Meanwhile, families all across this great country of ours stay cash poor.

Today, our personal financial instability is receiving national attention. Various groups and organizations are being formed to encourage Americans to save more and spend less. One of the newest programs is called America Saves, a nonprofit campaign managed by the Consumer Federation of America and supported by fifty national nonprofit groups, the government, and businesses. The goal is to get people all over American to reduce debt and increase savings.

The way things are going, this program couldn't be more appropriate. As the word gets around, hopefully, Americans will finally wake up and realize the importance of savings.

On the other hand, the idea of encouraging Americans to save is nothing new. Scores of books have been written on the topic; radios, magazines, and newspapers have tackled the issue in various ways; and in the last fifteen years, we've been inundated with information on personal finance from the Internet. Even so, the majority of Americans remain clueless about money management.

Could it be that most of the materials that are written on the subject of money have failed to address the real problem? Although this not entirely true, the idea has some merit. To my observation, most authors have taken the Band-Aid approach to solving this national epidemic. Let's face it. The issue goes beyond what is or isn't happening on Wall Street, whether or not most of us have a spending plan, our excessive spending habit, and our dependency on credit. Many of these issues are only symptoms of a bigger problem, one that's rooted deep in the fabric of our culture. And unless we tackle it at that level, the problem will continue to spread indefinitely.

Allow me to cite a personal experience. One day, I was scheduled to speak to a group of people who worked in the legal profession. As usual, I arrived early and got engaged in small talk with some of the group members. During the conversation, a gentleman walked up to me and said, "I hope you came by to give us the secret to financial success. I've read so many books on finance," he said, "hoping to find the *one thing* that will make a difference in my financial future. But unfortunately, I haven't been able to find it."

"That's too bad," I replied. "The bookstores have lots of books and magazine on the topic of finance. Granted, some of them may be more difficult to understand than others, especially for a person who is unfamiliar with the language of investments. At the same time, please understand that there's no *one thing* that I, or anyone else, can say to you that would instantly make your wish come true."

"The truth is," I continued, "financial success is not attained by knowing or doing *one thing*, but rather through the discovery of *many things* combined with a specific philosophy deliberately aimed at a desired financial outcome. In other words, you need to discover the things that are preventing you from attaining the wealth you desire. And when you find them and learn how to control them, wealth will come to you."

"Be advised," I said. "The answer to your pursuit may not necessarily come from a book, magazine, newspaper, or any other print media. But instead, part of the information you seek is around you, and the other part is inside you. So, in fact, you carry with you both the problem and the solution."

The gentleman, after listening to my reply, was somewhat perplexed. After mulling over what I said, he went and found a seat in the audience. My guess is that he was ready to hear what I had to say.

What about you? Are you looking for that *one thing* that will improve your financial disposition forever? If so, you must be cautious about where you look because while you're busy searching for that financial recipe, the answer could be closer than you think. In fact, much is imbedded within you—cultural customs or habits that have become part of your lifestyle.

In the following chapters, you will discover some of what I refer to as "cultural traps" designed to keep us broke. Many of them are customs or habits intended to improve our lives. Yet in many ways, they do more harm than good.

The following information is challenging and not intended for the narrow-minded person. Because when you become familiar with the cultural culprits that have hindered your financial progress, you may be surprised. In fact, your reaction could be one of many; you may find them to be convincingly amusing, personally probing, unbelievably surprising, and painfully truthful.

On the other hand, you may have the tendency to underestimate their influence, thinking that you can escape their gripping powers. For instance, if you're in your early twenties, you may be cocky enough to think that you've gotten everything under control. You may have seen your parents struggle with their finances and feel confident that you can overcome these issues in your own household. Your plan is to get into college or the military for a great start. After graduating from college or leaving the military, you anticipate getting a $60,000 to $70,000 job and retiring at age fifty-five.

However, the same cultural traps that snared your parents are set for you. And unless you know what they are and learn how to avoid them, they'll catch you too. In fact, what you may not realize is that you're currently being influenced by these traps and don't know it.

CHAPTER 6

Autoculture Kids, Youth and Money

(Cultural Trap No. 1)

From the day you were born, you started a journey from point "A" to point "B." Point "A" being the beginning of your life and "B," the end. As you start the journey, you were automatically attached to an imaginary timeline. This timeline counts the months and years of your life. Unlike an umbilical cord that usually gets severed during birth, this timeline cannot be cut. You're attached to it until you die.

In some ways, it may appear that you have little control over your circumstances as you take this trip. But that's not entirely so. Truly, as far as your birth was concerned, you had no say-so about it. The conditions in which you were born—e.g., choice of father, mother, place, time of day, etc.—were beyond your doing. Nonetheless, you've been given a lot of control to determine the quality of your life. You and you alone have the responsibility to shape the outcome of your life just the way you want it.

As you walk to your destination, keep in mind that nothing you do will come easy. You'll run into roadblocks designed to derail your mission, assuming, of course, you know where you're going. Let's step through the condition of your circumstances.

Childhood and Money

It is believed that children are influenced more by what they see than what they hear. One of the reasons is because human beings are more impressed by visual images than creative language. So children are more impressed by role models because, generally, their actions speak louder than what they say. You've heard it before: "Don't tell me, show me."

It is for this reason that child psychologists agree that most of our education takes place between zero and twelve years old (see figure 6.1).

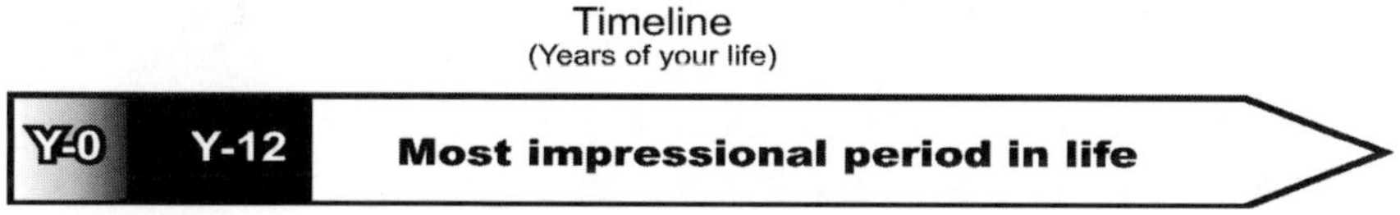

Timeline
(Years of your life)

| Y-0 | Y-12 | Most impressional period in life |

Fig. 6.1

During those years of life, we mimic just about everything we see. That include both good and bad habits from parents, friends, and others. Most often, these habits become the core of our being, forming a base for what is to come next.

For example, as early as one month old, your parents took you to the mall and supermarket to get you acquainted with the environment. As you got older, you realized that those trips meant something wonderful. In addition to being mesmerized by the variety of products on the shelves, you enjoyed receiving things such as toys, candy, food, etc., on the days you went shopping.

At age three and a half, you began expressing your opinions and wishes. At that age, studies show that about two-thirds of children begin to ask for things they see on television. And between ages four and a half to five years old, they start memorizing the locations of certain products in the store.

During those stages, you started learning survival techniques. The most effective one was the art of *manipulation*. One day it occurred to you that if you acted a certain way, your parents would respond to your needs in a positive fashion. So that behavior became a game, and you used it to your advantage to get what you wanted.

During that time, your parents still made purchasing decisions for you, but not for long. One study shows that after age four, parents give up control and allow their children to buy what they want.

From that point forward, children are recognized as major consumers in this country. Consequently, advertisers are increasingly bypassing parents and pitching their products directly to children.

Recent statistics show that American corporations spend in excess of $15 billion annually to advertise their products to children. This is twice the amount spent three decades ago.

When you were about six years old, the value of money became more real. You began understanding the various denominations of money, and spending made more sense.

By the time you were eight years old, your world of "stuff" had become much bigger. The candy aisle had expanded, and your toy selection got more expensive. So naturally, your desire for money grew more intense. As a result, you came up with creative ways such as doing chores around the house to earn it.

With the extra money came more independence. You started making your own purchasing decisions. Your favorite items were toys, burgers and fries, clothes, shoes, music, and more. When you couldn't pay for these things, you coaxed your parents into buying them for you. Today, children between the ages of four and twelve years old induce adult purchases in excess of $500 billion each year.

The amount of money American children generate in one year is staggering. Studies show that children between the ages of four and twelve years old have an annual income in excess of $17 billion (a figure mentioned earlier). Forty-six percent of that money comes from allowances, 20 percent comes from working around the house, 16 percent comes from parents as gifts, 10 percent comes from neighborly chores, and 8 percent is generated through friends and relatives.

By the way, of the $17 billion that children earn, they saved roughly $5.9 billion and spent approximately $11 billion. The spending portions are broken down as follow:

- $3.4 billion on candy, soft drinks, frozen desserts, fruit, and other snacks such as chips and popcorn
- $2.89 billion on toys, games, and crafts
- $2.21 billion on clothing
- $1.2 billion on movies, spectator sports, and live entertainment
- $900 million on video-arcade games
- $864 million on "other" expenditures: stereos, telephones, fragrances, cosmetics, cassettes, and compact discs

It would be nice to know that most of the $5.9 billion saved was placed in some type of long-term investment. But that's asking for too much. Most children simply haven't had the discipline to sustain such a saving habit. My guess is that most of the money eventually got spent.

Why? Few people are able to save money long-term without a plan. One must have a goal in mind, otherwise the money will be spent on the next attractive "thing." This is true for adults as well as children. Since most children are not thinking long-term, they're easily distracted by store, radio, magazine, and television advertisements. Therefore, with the right amount of pressure, even the most well-disciplined child will reach for the piggy bank and go shopping.

You, too, had similar problems with money while growing up. Not only did you have difficulty earning enough money, but you also struggled with the idea of saving some of what you earned. You may have taken steps to put away some money after your parents reprimanded you for excessive spending, but your desire to keep buying things controlled you. As a result, your savings never amounted to anything substantial. So you gave up on the idea, thinking that only grown-ups have the ability to put aside money. You decided to wait for adulthood to start saving.

During that phase of your life, you were simply doing what you saw others do. And since few people talked about money in those days, parents who saved part of their income did not tell the children. Thus, their children were excused from the attitude and discipline of saving. What they saw, instead, was a ceaseless pattern of spending. So while your parents may have encouraged you to set aside part of your income, they failed to *show* you how to do it.

Today, you may have the tendency to blame your parents for your financial ineptitude. But the fact remains that their financial knowledge may have been limited, too. And that's the point. Since financial management was an unmentionable subject, everyone kept silent about their savings. What few people realized was that the bad habit was being passed on to subsequent generations.

Unfortunately, the old financial secrecy still exists. Roughly 95 percent of children are leaving home without any knowledge about money except how to spend it. The question is, why do so many parents have difficulty educating their children about finance? The answer may be obvious to you, having experienced the problem firsthand.

The response I usually get from an audience is that most parents are financially illiterate.

This answer parallels what experts have believed all along. Most parents avoid talking to their children about money for the following reasons: (1) a need to maintain privacy, (2) the topic is generally too complicated for open discussion, (3) embarrassment surrounding the lack of financial progress, and (4) few people have practiced the personal discipline that they preached to their children. So you and your friends grew up being financially illiterate as well.

Granted, you knew what a twenty-dollar bill was. You understood how much change to expect after purchasing an item. But that may have been the extent of your financial knowledge. And frankly, as a child, you cared less about knowing any more. What you didn't know was that this problem would eventually come back to disturb you.

Teens and Money

The general assumption is that as we grow up, we automatically gain financial knowledge. But that's far from the truth. One does not become financially smart by virtue of age. Financial know-how takes both discipline and practice, something that becomes part of a person as the individual gets older. And if those two components are missed in the lives of children, when the time comes to make financial decisions, they'll naturally fall back on old habits. Studies show that young people demonstrate the same careless spending habits during the time of thirteen and nineteen years old (see figure 6.2).

Timeline
(Years of your life)

Fig. 6.2

A national survey of 2,020 young people, ages twelve through nineteen, revealed a continued tendency to spend on things of little intrinsic value:

- 15 percent bought stereo equipment
- 12 percent bought radios
- 11 percent bought in-home CD players
- 10 percent bought stereos with headphones
- 7 percent bought video-games systems
- 6 percent bought portable CD players
- 5 percent bought personal computers

The problem is further amplified even on a scholastic level. A 2002 survey found twelfth graders flunking a financial literary test. In a group of 4,025 high-school seniors, the average score was 50.2 percent on a thirty-one-question multiple-choice examination. Two years prior, 722 students participated in a similar examination and scored an average of 51.9 percent. And in 1997, the result of a similar test was 57.4 percent.

Clearly, there seems to be a major disconnection in the minds of young Americans when it comes to dealing with money and financial concepts. But who's at fault? Should we blame the parents, the teachers, the schools, the students, or all of the above? Based on what we've discussed so far, the answer is simple: all of us are guilty (the culture). We have failed in the financial education department. We've undermined the value of money by simply associating it with nothing more than spending. Beyond that, the whole issue becomes blurry. And in critical moments, where financial prudence is necessary, most of us cannot survive.

But don't tell American teenagers that they need to learn about money management. They know all there is to know about the subject. Yet when it comes to a topic such as investments, they're lost. It's a foreign language, a topic that belongs only in the media. Moreover, the banking system remains a mystery. Few young Americans understand the concept of banking. Additionally, check writing and account reconciliation are absolutely meaningless to them.

Meanwhile, parents assume that their young adults will do well in life, especially if they have a college degree. But it doesn't take long before this assumption proves them wrong. In spite of the college degree, those who missed financial training from home soon find themselves making bad financial decisions.

For instance, credit card companies are turning college campuses into profit centers. And why not? The students are financially naive and gullible. Consequently, it's not surprising to see college graduates walking away from campus with an average of $12,000 in credit card debt. The irony is, they are supposed to be much smarter than the rest of us, a frightening revelation.

Unfortunately, this global economic system is apathetic to financial ignorance. Even those with good financial sense are finding it difficult to stay solvent. Therefore, those who are less prepared will have a much harder time surviving. One simply cannot bluff his or her way through the economic maze and hope to make it big. In addition to having financial astuteness, a person needs unwavering tenacity, both of which are severely lacking in today's youth.

The culture needs to change its attitude about financial issues. If not, millions of Americans will remain financially illiterate, a condition which invites ongoing poverty. This is a sad commentary for a culture which prides itself on educating the young. Yet it trivializes the only topic in the world that makes sense: financial education.

Today, regardless how old you are, this is the environment in which you grew up and now live. Because you missed having proper financial education and training, this oversight on the part of your parents has impeded your financial progress. One can only assume that if you had learned good money management skills early and had practiced them all through your adolescent period, your chances of success would have increased greatly.

Sadly, unless you alter your view about money and start changing your saving and spending habits, things will stay the same.

Recommendations to Parents

No other subject in school is more important to a child than financial education. While history, sociology, geometry, and even math and English are essential building blocks for a complete education, they should be secondary subjects when compared to the fundamentals of money management.

We've all seen the smart people of the world. Those who can recall any historical event, prove any mathematical theory, send people to the moon, and run large corporations. Yet many of them can't manage their personal finances. In this culture, we teach people how to find a job, make money, spend it, and get into debt. But we provide them little or no education and training on how to "keep" some of the money they make.

But then again, the subject of money management is not a job for the schools, but the responsibility of parents. While the schools may support the concept, children need tangible financial application. They need to be *shown* how to earn money, how to value it, how to apply it, and how to maximize its capacity. The home is the only place where this can be done properly.

Therefore, without disclosing important information about account balances, parents need to *demonstrate* (not tell) to children as early as three years old the concept of money management in real time. Meaning, children need to see and apply the art of finance in the following areas:

- *Check writing,* including the purpose for which the check is written and the amount.
- *Personal savings,* to include the practice of setting the money aside, walking into the bank, and making a deposit. If the transaction is done on a computer, the child needs to witness the transfer. Additionally, parents need to explain to children the benefit of saving and investing money.
- *Personal "commitment" to savings,* to include a steady commitment to putting some money away regardless how small. A monthly ritual would be perfect. If this is carried out, not only will they have some money at the end of the year, but they'll also develop the discipline necessary for future success.
- *Personal control,* to include resisting the urge to use saved money except for emergencies or planned spending.
- *Impulsive spending,* that means resisting the urge to purchase an item on the spur of the moment just becomes it feels or looks good. Television commercials, paper advertisements, and supermarket displays are intended to entice our fancy and make us buy on the spot. Fight the temptation by walking away.
- *The use of a credit card,* using it only when absolutely necessary. And even then, exercise prudence.

Honestly, the ineffectual method of telling children what to do about money should be stopped. Instead, they need to "see" a consistent set of positive, financial discipline such as saving part of one's earnings each month.

CHAPTER 7

Autoculture Beliefs, Values and Money

(Cultural Trap No. 2)

You've heard the saying—"You're a product of your culture"—a statement that will ring true for as long humanity exists. The way you were raised, specifically what you were taught to believe and practice as a child, was directly influenced by your surroundings.

You were *programmed* while growing up. Information came from various sources—friends, neighbors, schoolteachers, pastors, and so on, all of whom have been influenced by the culture itself and passing, more or less, the same information onto you.

Since you haven't been evenly exposed to these influences, it's fair to say that one or more had greater power over you than the other. This is certainly true for all of us.

The critical aspect of this is not necessarily who or what influenced you more, but rather the type of information you received. For example, it's possible for children to do well in school, particularly in the arts and sciences, and continue to excel in those areas as adults yet still fail to achieve financial success. In this case, the problem is not necessarily a question of good or bad education, but more a question of other types of influences such as personal beliefs and values.

If you're not making financial progress, it may be necessary to examine how you're *programmed*. The reality is, you might be encoded for a different purpose or mission. In which case, you would be getting a different set of results than you expected. Can you imagine, for example, someone desiring to go to the moon and being encoded for Venus or Mars? The end results would be extremely disappointing.

The same could be said about financial success. Some people carry bad concepts of money while looking for clues to be rich.

The Impact of Beliefs and Values

A *belief,* as you know, is an opinion, a point of view regarding a specific concept such as freedom, education, happiness, respect, politics, security, and so on. It could also include opinions of particular groups such as government, corporations, churches, schools, etc.

Values, on the other hand, have to do with the measure of importance you place on each of these concepts or groups. For instance, you may score a concept such as *respect* higher than *security* because of the way you were raised and what you were taught as a child. School may hold a more prominent position in your mind than government. So, at a critical moment of choice between any of these two situations, you will favor one over the other.

The thing to realize is that your set of beliefs and values are yours and yours alone. Given the same set of circumstances, another person may choose just the opposite, placing more value on *security* than *respect.* Yet the choices are neither right nor wrong. The only important factor is the outcome of each decision.

And that's the point. Since our culture measures progress, financial or otherwise, based on *outcome,* a positive mindset is crucially important to achieving a positive outcome. This is true for those who work in government, business enterprises, sports groups, military outfits, home life, or those who work in any other endeavors. Thus, since our beliefs and values ultimately dictate our outcomes, knowing what we believe and why, is extremely important to our mission. This is certainly true in the world of finance.

For that reason, part of your responsibility is to determine whether or not you're carrying excess baggage from past or present generations: bad programming codes that were once dumped into your memory. If that's the case, they could be obstructing your financial progress. You may benefit by discarding them completely.

Building the courage to do this could be challenging, however. Walking away from a specific comfort, habit, or belief is not necessarily the easiest thing in the world, especially when it relates to well-established family customs. Nevertheless, you have the choice of replacing the old, negative customs or beliefs with new, positive ones. Otherwise, the old ones will continue dominating your outcome negatively.

To make sense of this, we need to fall back on a few well-known situations. We'll briefly visit the belief and value system of four American generations regarding money. The goal is to identify a specific financial philosophy, trait, or attitude within each group. While doing so, you should also examine the reason behind each belief and value system. During the process, try to line up your own thinking against theirs to see how you compare. My guess is that you may find a few parallels.

The Great Depression Group

Born between 1912 and 1921, these individuals turned eighteen years old between 1930 and 1939. Impacted by The Great Depression of the 1930s, they became survivalists. Consequently, they valued *security* as their number one priority and believed that it could be attained by having a lot of money.

As a result, The Great Depression survivalists made saving money a priority. Since their recent tragedy served as a constant reminder of wastefulness and excessive spending, they were bent in the opposite direction. They only spent money for their needs. Furthermore, in addition to influencing their children to do the same thing, they also felt morally responsible to transfer wealth to them, ensuring their comfort and safety in the future.

Looking at this group, there is nothing strange about their approach. It's only natural for humans to protect themselves, especially after going through a disaster like The Great Depression. In fact, I'm reminded of the story in the Bible where men started building a great tower several hundred feet high to reach heaven (The Tower of Babel). The group was afraid of the next worldwide flood that would eventually come and destroy them since the previous flood had covered the entire earth, killing every living thing except Noah, his family, and one pair of every creature on the earth. Having witnessed this experience, the survivalists wanted to protect themselves in the future from a similar disaster.

Fortunately, the Tower of Babel never got finished. After several years of hard work, the people were forced to abandon the project because God had intervened. He changed their original language to something different, creating a communication chaos. Confused and frustrated, those who understood each other walked away to build their own colonies. Consequently, the Tower project was abandoned forever. Interestingly enough, since that major flood, the planet has never experienced anything like it.

The Great Depression group took a similar approach in dealing with their experience. Based on their knowledge of their recent tragedy, they anticipated something equal or worse in the future. Naturally, they wanted to minimize their vulnerability against any unfriendly surprises. So they concluded that lots of money would solve any potential problem. Therefore, they attempted to save as much of it as possible to avert any future catastrophe.

Whether or not a similar occurrence happened is irrelevant in this situation. The point here is to focus on a specific attitude of a group and what caused it. In this case, their mission was to conserve money. They became somewhat obsessed with the idea, hoping to prevent a major embarrassment in the future.

The World War II Cohorts

The World War II group lived in a dichotomous world. They believed that prosperity could be attained by saving money. But they also believed that individual spending was important to prove *prominence* in society. So they demonstrated two separate belief systems: their parents' savings concept and contemporary influence.

Born between 1922 and 1927, this group became young adults between 1940 and 1945. Having gone through The Great Depression and the war as children, they were unified by a common experience. Additionally, they became intensely romantic and self-serving. As far as they were concerned, the penny-pinching attitude they experienced as children was a thing of the past. They wanted a better life for themselves and their children.

Of course, this attitude led the group in an entirely new direction, one that encouraged more spending and, ultimately, a robust economy. In the process, some people became extremely wealthy, giving them extra leverage in the community. Those who could afford to spend bought luxurious homes, comfortable automobiles, expensive apparel, and better services. As a result, they were treated with respect and dignity over those with less.

Those who desired the affluent lifestyle but couldn't afford it kept spending anyway. They were determined to create the comfortable setting they had imagined. This attitude eventually gave birth to the credit concept, a method by which one purchases an item without money and pays the bill later. This method of shopping was convenient, fun, and easy, which led people to spend more than they would otherwise spend with cash.

This overspending habit eventually created additional problems for impulsive spenders, however. Most of their disposable income got tied up in debt payments, leaving them less cash for savings.

Meanwhile, concern for the future became less important. Not only did this group save less money for their own retirement, but also felt less responsible to transfer wealth to their children. Again, they practiced a different set of habits than their parents, establishing an entirely new behavior that would carry its own set of consequences in the future.

The Postwar Generation

Born between 1928 and 1945, the postwar children became adults between 1946 and 1963. Growing up during a period of economic bliss and tranquility, they felt no threat about the future. So they valued peace of mind.

They, too, anticipated a life of security and comfort. However, unlike their parents who placed heavy emphasis on spending more for present comfort, the postwar generation was a little more levelheaded. They believed that money should be prudently distributed between spending and saving. To them, a person could spend as much as he or she wanted as long as a portion of income was set aside for retirement.

Unfortunately, time would eventually test their resolve. After the war, the economy gradually got stronger, thus, creating an atmosphere where everyone felt more secure about the general prosperity of the nation. With little on their minds, the postwar group gradually shifted their attention from moderate savings to heavy spending. By doing so, they signaled a general attitude of wealth, good times, and prosperity. Ultimately, they became bigger spenders than their parents.

The Boomers

The boomer generation was born between 1946 and 1965 and became adults between 1963 and 1983. In many ways, this group was different because they walked through an array of unique cultural experiences. They witnessed a booming economy, an illegal-drug explosion, two presidential assassinations, and a free-sex revolution. Additionally, they witnessed the war in Vietnam, the Watergate fiasco, and the *Apollo 13* moon landing.

In spite of national turmoil, the boomers enjoyed a life of convenience. They valued comfort as a way of life and believed that it should be achieved by any means possible, including going into debt. Consequently, they spent most of their lives in a cycle of borrowing and spending.

Ultimately, this cyclical borrowing habit became synonymous with the boomers. Since they remained cash poor most of the time, their credit dependency gave rise to the term "buy now and pay later," a popular theme with that generation.

Until this era, credit was reserved for those who could clearly show means of repaying the debt. In time, however, the boomers devised sophisticated methods of lending and borrowing, making it possible for anyone to qualify for credit.

This liberal credit approach gave rise to other cultural problems. Millions of people got into the habit of spending excessively, creating additional financial complications for themselves and others.

Even so, the credit system flourished in spite of these issues. The boomers were simply motivated by *comfort,* and they were willing achieve it by any method possible, even though it meant ignoring sound financial judgment.

The Generation X'ers

According to experts, the Generation X'ers were totally confused when it came to dealing with money. Like the generation before them, not only did they not have good financial training, but they also lacked good role models.

This group was born between 1966 and 1976 and became adults between 1984 and 1994. Raised by parents who were self-absorbed, they witnessed careless spending that left them with negative impressions about money. Since their parents created huge amounts of debt in the pursuit of *pleasure* and *comfort,* they experienced firsthand the consequences of bad financial judgment and excessive spending.

For example, this group gave rise to the term "home alone," suggesting neglect or abandonment. As a result of both parents working, they witnessed family evictions, separations, misplaced priorities, divorces, bankruptcies, and a host of other negative cultural issues such as single parenting, day-care centers, latchkey kids, and more. Most of these issues, of course, were directly or indirectly associated with money.

According to social experts, this group is unsure whether it's coming or going. They have become cynical, cautious, conservative, and untrusting. They remain aloof, and they question everything. Before they get involved in something, they want to see tangible benefits. Otherwise, they want no part of it. Thus, they live by the motto, "What's in it for me?"

Generation X'ers believe in *security* and *permanence.* However, they lack the confidence to tie both together for stability. Their parents' inability to handle money provided no positive memory. Yet their lack of financial knowledge hinders their confidence to move forward. So they resort to an indecisive posture when dealing with saving and spending. They're confused.

Today, sociologists believe that X'ers are lacking a center or midpoint in the lifes. They can't relate to the past and they remain dubious about the future. Furthermore, since they haven't experienced a Great Depression, a national war, or a major conflict—until the recent chaos of September 11, 2002, and the ongoing conflict in Afghanistan and Iraq—they're convinced that all national problems are directly related to the irresponsible actions of previous generations. Moreover, while they condemn their parents' and grandparents' ways of handling money, they have no successful system of their own.

An Assessment

Whatever you're thinking at this point regarding these brief historical perspectives, one thing to keep in mind is that the brushes that painted these pictures considered only the mainstream or the majority. In light of this, it's reasonable to assume that there were people (families) on opposite sides of the spectrum. As such, my guess is that they had their own financial philosophy.

Recalling the circumstances of each generation, you may have noticed that each one developed its own viewpoint regarding money. They did so by maintaining a portion of their parents' beliefs while combining them with a new set of philosophies. In the end, they created a brand-new concept branding each generation with a unique title.

It's interesting to note that starting with The Great Depression group, things got progressively worse financially for subsequent generations. As the economy got better, people spent more money, resulting in less money to save in the process. Seemingly, in just about every situation, immediate *needs* and *wants* took precedence over concerns for the future, leaving them financially vulnerable in their old age.

Today, many of these people are our parents, grandparents, and great-grandparents. How are they doing financially? The truth is, millions of them are depending on some type of financial assistance from government, charitable groups, and their own children. Currently, 23 million families provide some type of financial care for elders. The most painful aspect of this is that 64 percent of caregivers are holding jobs. One would have to be in this type of situation only briefly to know what it feels like.

The question is, how are you lining up with all of this? Did you see yourself in one or a combination of these scenarios? Realistically, every one of us can associate with one financial philosophy or another. And what we believe is either tangling us in a web of confusion or leading us toward progress. Your job is to determine whether or not your belief system is propelling you in the direction you want to go.

For all we know, financial issues are very sensitive and personal. As such, some people (families) harbor strange concepts about money, which are usually passed down to the next generation. Yet, not all of them are positive, healthy, and uplifting. In fact, some customs, rituals, or beliefs are very negative, depressing, and destructive. Therefore, it is possible that you're carrying both positive and negative ideas, thoughts, and beliefs everywhere you go.

What you may not realize is that your mission and beliefs may be contradicting each other and working against you. For that reason, as you try to move forward with your plan, your negative thinking may be getting in your way, destroying the very initiative you need to succeed.

For instance, a family who has struggled for years financially may easily find comfort in a statement from the Bible that says, "For the love of money is the root of all evil." Certainly, this view may not necessarily be shared by everybody in a generational group. Yet this belief can become the driving influence in one family, and ultimately gets passed down to the next generation.

As harmless as this statement or belief may appear to be, it carries fundamental consequences. Those who believe it are not only predisposed to financial poverty, but they're also likely to believe that those who possess wealth are automatically evil.

Moreover, they may also *conclude* that wealth leads to unhappiness, suggesting that people who have money are naturally unhappy. Otherwise, the only people that could possibly be happy are the poor, disadvantaged, and those who live from paycheck to paycheck. Consequently, since excessive wealth makes people bad, evil, or unhappy, they want no part of it, sabotaging their own financial success in the process.

A similar situation exists with those who've seen no extraordinary financial success in their immediate families. As such, they're unlikely to be motivated toward financial success, thinking that the entire family is cursed. Accordingly, they make no extra effort to achieve financial success. "What's the use?" they say. "We were born poor, and we'll die poor." They think nothing has worked in the past; therefore, nothing will work now.

This outlook on life is like a cancer that eats away at the brain cells. Slowly, it gradually chips away people's confidence, motivation, and initiative. Yet strangely enough, they wonder why they haven't made progress in life. This belief is likely to be passed down to the next generation, poisoning them as well.

In contrast, it's fair to assume that within each of the previous generations, some families (a minority) adopted a different financial philosophy, one that's more positive and encouraging in nature. A family who has experienced financial success in past generations is likely to believe that they can be successful. The same could be said about people who believe that they can attain financial success regardless of prior situations.

It is this type of positive view on life that makes a positive difference in the world. It transforms people and things from ordinary to extraordinary. And while it's true that nothing in life is guaranteed, it's not hard to predict that these people will be successful. Generally, they are the ones who become extremely wealthy and end up creating jobs for others.

It is believed that the human spirit has the capacity to accomplish anything it desires. Therefore, people who are infused with positive ideas, concepts, or beliefs at any age, but particularly as children, are fortunate. Their minds become incubators for seeds of greatness. And with the right tools, they're likely to produce positive results in their lives. Those, on the other hand, who are encouraged to believe negatively are less likely to have an abundance of positive results. In reality, as hard as they try to generate positive outcomes, their thinking generally leads them in an entirely different direction, creating ongoing frustration.

Recommendations for You

Science supports the fact that you and I have been influenced by culture, e.g., parents, friends, schools, and so on. What you are today has a great deal to do with what you were exposed to as a child and young adult. What you become is, ultimately, up to you.

The world is full of ideas from one extreme to another. Most of them are free. As such, you may have been infected by some of them like a virus in a computer, and chances are, you may need to purge your mind.

For all we know, there is a direct correlation to where you are today and your thinking. So, in the next few days or months, you may want to examine your belief and value systems and see whether or not they're supporting your mission. If you find some to be counterproductive to your goals, you may want to discard them. Here are some areas of concern for your consideration:

- *Self-pity*—Disregard things such as your poor background, your disadvantaged childhood, your present condition, and your lack of resources (education, money, time, etc). The past is the past, and you can't change it. But you can do something about the future. Create your own environment.

- *Procrastination*—You've heard it before, "Don't put off until tomorrow what you can do today." If you have a tendency to procrastinate, stop it! This bad habit will keep you broke for the rest of your life. It will kill your initiative, rob your time, delay your progress, and put you at the back of the line.

- *Excuses*—Bring an end to justifying every mistake or negative condition in your life. No one really cares, and you come across as weak, pathetic, and indecisive.

- *Complaints*—Stop complaining about conditions in life. Situations or circumstances will never be exactly right for you or anyone else, for that matter. You have to create your desired outcome.

- *Customs*—Disregard old family habits that waste time, produce little or no long-term results, or seem useless.

- *Beliefs and values*—Examine your thinking pattern. Observe your attitude about religion, money, success, wealth, friends, family, and relatives. If they are impeding your progress, make changes.

- *Organization*—Organize your bank accounts, important papers, garages, closets, desks, etc. When these areas of your life are put in order, your mind starts thinking in a linear fashion.

- *Chance, good fortune, and luck*—Don't believe in these things because they don't exist. People who believe in them don't accomplish much in life. They wait on others to do for them, and nothing gets done.

- *Gambling*—Avoid gambling. Those who do it are betting on their last luck, and they generally walk away feeling disappointed and still broke.

Those are some of many negative ideas that can hamper your success in life. After eradicating them from your memory, you must fill the void with healthy, productive concepts that will move you forward. Consider these:

- *Believe in your ability*—You are capable of doing much more than you think. If you believe in yourself, anything is possible.

- *Take risks*—Nothing gets done without taking risks. All great and successful people had to sacrifice something—time, money, and reputation to achieve their goals.
- *Cultivate good friendships*—Find people who are positive and making a difference in the community and offer your friendship to them. You'll be enriched with their wisdom.
- *Avoid complainers and whiners*—These people are generally negative, energy-drainers who drag themselves and others down into self-pity.
- *Befriend a successful person*—Most successful people are generally positive and can't wait to share their secret to success with someone who is eager to win. Use those people as mentors.
- *Have faith in a higher being*—A lot of people find comfort in God or another higher being. This a good way to build your faith and hope in life.
- *Take action, now*—One of the best ways to overcome fear and procrastination is to take action. Whatever you need to do, follow through on it right away. Tomorrow is not promised.
- *Admit your weaknesses to yourself, spouse, and children*—those who are able to do this develop strength and character through the process.

Applying these concepts may not be easy for you. The truth is, you might be set in your ways and don't want to change for anyone. Well, keep in mind that if you have children, watching you change might make a positive difference in their lives. And for you, it could be an improvement in your destiny.

CHAPTER 8

Autoculture Education

(Cultural Trap No. 3)

"Go to college," we say, "find a good job, work hard, and you'll get ahead." This was, and still is, the American formula for financial success. But does it really work? How reliable is this success recipe, anyway? Millions of Americans have followed this plan step by step, hoping to be rich before or by retirement age. Instead, they became bitterly disappointed in the end. The well-promoted blueprint to success is lacking muscle and remains questionable, at best.

The popular view is still widely accepted as the pathway to financial success. So much so that millions of Americans continue to flood colleges and universities all across the country, hoping to "make it big" after graduation. Government figures show a steady increase in college and university enrollment between 1970 and 2010 (see figure 8.1).

Unfortunately, many of these people won't discover the flaw in the system until they graduate and start working. Years later, they'll look back and wonder what happened as they compare the costs and benefits of their efforts.

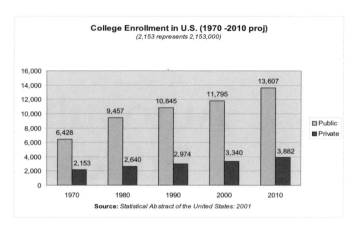

Fig. 8.1

The College Mandate

No one can deny the value of a good education. Knowledge in the field of science, business, government, and social issues is fundamental to a balanced view on life. Knowledge empowers people. In addition to stimulating the mind, those who are well-informed become resourceful, creative, and inspiring.

But knowledge is not necessarily acquired in one place. It comes from various sources. Therefore, one doesn't necessarily have to attend college to become smart. In fact, many of the great leaders, planners, and thinkers of our country had only a high school diploma or less. Most of them were self-educated visionaries. As such, academic achievement was simply a by-product. The following are people you may recognize:

- Thomas Edison
- Abraham Lincoln
- Frederick Douglass
- Alexander Graham Bell
- Henry Ford
- The Wright Brothers
- Charles Lindbergh
- Walt Disney
- Chuck Yeager
- Bill Gates

- Steve Jobs
- Kirk Kerkorian
- Harry Wayne Huizenga

Today, the majority of Americans believe that unless they go to college, they won't get ahead in life. It's as though the college degree itself is the magical tool to greatness. In fact, current attitude seems to imply that people are unable to intelligently think, plan, and initiate anything without a college degree, and that until they successfully achieve the credential, they're insignificant and helpless.

Those who are looking for someone to blame for this mindset should look no further than the culture, more specifically, schools, government, businesses, churches, and even parents. The concept is simple. Because the majority of us depend on others for employment, we're also subject to being controlled by them. For instance, over the years, employers have been exposed to increased competition in business. In response, they're imposing requirements on their employees, forcing them to seek more education and training.

The assumption is that after people graduate from college, they're automatically smarter. They're able to work in teams, follow directions, comply with government regulations, promote diversity, and support the company's culture.

The irony is, of course, most Americans believe that they're smart enough to adapt to any job requirement without a college degree. In fact, there are millions of people in this country with no more than a high school diploma, yet their intelligence surpasses those with higher education. But that's not the point. To make it fair to all, it's politically correct to mandate a college degree for a salary higher than minimum wage. Today, people who had no intention of attending college are being pressured to comply with the program, the cost of which is astronomical. Yet, if they decline the option of going to college, they're likely to lose their jobs to someone with a college degree.

"Doesn't that make sense?" you say. "This type of requirement should motivate everyone to attend college. After graduation, one is more likely to get a better job and make more money. Isn't that the point?"

Well, that depends on what you see when you look at the big picture. My hope is that by the time you get to the end of this chapter, you'll understand.

An Idea Hitting Home

Like millions of Americans who have complied with the college-degree stipulation, I made my way to college. My intent, though personal in some way, was to become competitive in the job market. But my experience both before and after graduation is one worth telling.

For what it's worth, few people will ever experience an equal or greater postgraduation thrill than mine. Immediately after receiving my diploma, I was psychologically transformed from one social class into another. I suddenly felt taller, richer, and more important. I was no longer a peon at the bottom of the ladder, but one who was suddenly grouped with the movers and shakers of the world: the bright people who knew where they were going and how to get there—or so I thought. I was proud of my accomplishment.

At this point, you might be thinking that there's nothing earth-shattering about a simple college graduation. This is something that happens every day, and most people are accustomed to it. In which case, I overreacted. That may be true. But to me, it was more than a milestone—it was a transformation.

For in many ways, I was the guy who would most likely *not* go to college. And if I did, I would most likely fail. I had no grade-school education; the arithmetic, the reading, the writing, and so on, were all missing until my early twenties. Furthermore, any recollection of a classroom experience was nothing less than disdain. During my first two years in school as a child, I was beaten, humiliated, and labeled as a dummy. Therefore, I avoided school as early as eight years old.

As I grew older, however, I began to realize the value of an education and envied those around me who could read and write. As a result, I became hungry for knowledge. In time, I began to wish I could go back to school. Yet, in a real way, I couldn't see myself sitting in a classroom again. Not only did I lack the knowledge and discipline to learn, but I also missed the opportunity of a lifetime. I was too old, I thought.

As mentioned earlier, I was nineteen years old when I started my school adventure. Since my age precluded me from sitting in a second-grade classroom, I was made to study in a private room to avoid embarrassment. Two years later, I received a ninth grade certificate and went on to pursue a full high school diploma.

Shortly thereafter, I started charting a course for my financial independence. Years later, I made my way to college. Sitting in a university classroom for the first time, I was overwhelmed by emotions. I wept because I was totally shocked that I had made it this far. That evening, I scanned the environment—the room, the instructor, the students, the desks, the green board, and so on. Suddenly, I realized that this place looked familiar—it was a scene from one of my going-back-to-school dreams except this time, it was real.

Throughout most of the evening, I had doubts about graduation. To this point, I had managed to come through high school, but I questioned my ability to do college work. Can I do it? I wondered. That evening, I convinced myself that it was possible and that I should do everything in my power to make this dream a reality.

Looking back on the experience, I was the perfect student. I attended every classroom session on time, did all of my required homework, and submitted all of my assignments by the deadline. In fact, one evening, I left my new bride in a hotel room during our honeymoon and went to school, an event she'll neither forgive nor forget.

I must say, however, that in spite of my commitment and efforts, college work didn't come easy. Some courses were extremely difficult to the point of frustration. There were times I regretted ever starting the process and wanted to bail out. Nevertheless, I kept on. Four years later, I graduated with a Bachelor of Science degree in business administration.

Today, I'm writing to you, but the path to get here wasn't easy either. For what it's worth, I'm the ambitious type who's always looking for ways to make life easier. And so, like everyone else, I went to college to earn a degree, which would eventually help me make a lot of money to create a hassle-free, stress-free lifestyle.

What I didn't know was that my biggest challenge was still ahead, circumstances that would end up changing my life forever. For instance, all through school, I worked as a computer technician and enjoyed the work. However, my heart was in the field of business. I liked the planning, the accounting, the marketing, and all the rest of the excitement that came with being in business. Therefore, shortly after graduation, I began looking for work in that field, thinking that I was well qualified to handle any type of business situation.

But finding a job became a job in itself. Mind you, I wasn't ignorant about the process of seeking and finding work. I was currently employed and had other jobs prior to this one. But this search was especially difficult. Though I had management, supervisory, and bookkeeping experience, I spent approximately four months looking for a suitable job—anything that would pay a decent wage. But to my dismay, I was blatantly ignored in broad daylight. I experienced age discrimination, over-qualification gobbledygook, lack of qualification, and minority issues.

Disappointed and confused, I decided to continue working as a computer technician and return to school for a master's degree in business. My hope was that the advanced degree would give me the edge I needed to succeed.

But making that decision wasn't easy, either. Going back to school meant piling up additional debt, something I feared from the beginning. So far, I had accumulated roughly $40,000 in student loans, an amount of money that scared the daylights out of me. A graduate degree would probably double the sum. Nonetheless, after tossing the idea around for about a month, I enrolled in the same university for a graduate degree. My thought was, if it took a graduate degree to break down the barriers I experienced, I would get one.

Two years later, I graduated with a Master's Degree in organization management. I was thrilled. However, the experience was nothing close to my first graduation ecstasy. Life had become more real. I had accumulated roughly $75,000 in student loans, and I began to have doubts whether or not I would ever pay off that debt.

On the other hand, I had confidence in the fact that my newly acquired master's degree would provide the financial means by which to pay my debt. Surely, I'll be able to get a job with no problem—at least so I thought. In fact, this time, the ball was in my court, and I could be choosy if necessary.

The weeks following graduation, I approached the job market with a renewed attitude. Mentally, my chances had increased significantly because of the higher credential. But I was wrong. It didn't take me long to start running into job discrimination again. And though I tried to ignore the signs, they were too obvious to miss.

For instance, while looking for work one day, I made a comment about my college degree to someone I respected. After listening to me, the person responded in a way I didn't expect. "Tom," she said with a serious tone and fixating eyeball, "no one cares about your degrees." When she made the statement, she walked away allowing me time to ponder what she had said.

To say the least, her statement shot through me like a bullet, leaving me gasping for breath. Visibly, I was fine, but I felt sick to my stomach by her statement. As I walked away, I felt insignificant once again.

It took me days to heal from my acquaintance's comment, but I eventually felt well again and continued my search for work. Approximately three months later, still struggling to find a job, I requested the assistance of a job-placement agency. During my first interview with the company, I ran into an additional revelation that stunned me even more.

"Tom," said the interviewer, "you have an impressive résumé. It shows that you possess great skills in management, planning, organizing, and leadership. The format is good, and everything is well written. Furthermore, I see you as a team player, good listener, and good communicator. You also dress well, and you're full of energy and fire. All of these are admirable traits, which are coveted by most employers. But you have one problem."

"What's that?" I asked. "Your age," he replied. "You're 45 years old, and a lot of companies shun the idea of hiring older job candidates in favor of the younger twenty-somethings right out of college." My body went cold as I came to grips with the reality of my situation. Frankly, it was hard to accept the fact that my chances in life were gone. Pondering my fate in that office, I thought about the time, money, and effort I spent getting those degrees. "Why wasn't I made aware of this age problem while going to school?" I asked myself. And more importantly, "How am I going to pay off the $75,000 student loan I accumulated in the process?"

Then, I thought about my fellow students. Were they in the same predicament? Most of them were about my age and loaded with debt, just like me. Or was I experiencing an isolated problem?

There were no answers. And more poignantly, no one cared. In the minds of potential employers, my degree had no value and was, therefore, meaningless. Besides, since I had passed the point of productivity, I had become more of a liability than an asset to a company in fierce competition.In time, however, I found work in a field I didn't expect: finance.

Looking back on my experience, I haven't regretted the decision of going to college. If for no other reason, I proved to myself that I had the capacity to learn just like anyone else. Since then, however, I've come to realize that those who depend on a college degree as a way to financial success may want to rethink their strategies.

Pregraduation Expectations

It's not uncommon for college students to sit in sanitized class-rooms with distorted expectations about the real world. Those of us who've gone through college know that the campus environment has a tendency to distort reality. In fact, four to six years of thumbing through textbooks, doing case studies, and listening to lectures is a lot of time to dream about solutions to all kinds of political, social, and economic issues in this country. Life, on the other hand, is completely different when one leaves the campus and steps into the real world.

The same is true of the money issue. Recent surveys show that potential MBA students are looking forward to making large sums of money right after graduation. Those enrolled in top universities around the country believe that they'll be able to command $100,000 the first year following graduation, $200,000 in five years, and $300,000 in ten years.

Wishful thinking? Maybe not. Based on 2001 *Statistical Abstract of the United States,* this type of income is possible. In 1999, professionals made a little more than $100,000 in annual income on the average. Those with higher degrees (Master's and PhD's) also generated a high-average salary during that period (see figure 8.2).

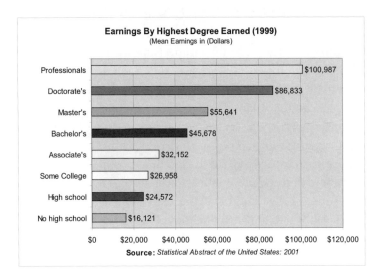

Earnings By Highest Degree Earned (1999)
(Mean Earnings in (Dollars))

Professionals	$100,987
Doctorate's	$86,833
Master's	$55,641
Bachelor's	$45,678
Associate's	$32,152
Some College	$26,958
High school	$24,572
No high school	$16,121

$0 $20,000 $40,000 $60,000 $80,000 $100,000 $120,000

Source: *Statistical Abstract of the United States: 2001*

Fig. 8.2

Postgraduation Realism

There is no question that those who go to college have a greater income potential than those who don't. The Census Bureau estimated that college graduates will earn roughly 73 percent more income over their lifetime than high-school graduates.

Again, the previous graph provides all the evidence we need to support this fact. In that study, the top 10 percent of the group made roughly $316,000 a year. These individuals were people with years of experience who worked as lawyers, physicians, and other high-level executives. No doubt, some MBA students will have the same opportunity to make this type of income five to ten years after graduation.

The problem arises when most MBA graduates expect to earn this kind of money. The truth is, only 10 percent of graduate students earn a $300,000 annual income. The rest of them make much less.

But the income issue is only part of the problem that graduates or undergraduates encounter. As many of us have found out, there are many political, social, and economic factors that impede an individual's progress. Yet these factors are usually ignored or overlooked prior to enrolling in college.

The Diminishing Job Market

According to information from the National Center for Education Statistics, 1.9 million people were awarded bachelor's degrees in 1998 compared to 934,800 in 1981. This growth was attributed to women and older people who felt the need to go back to school.

For these people, the reason for going to college was more than attaining bragging rights. They were driven by the need to earn more money. Historical trends have indicated that most people are interested in employment immediately after graduation. The Bureau of Labor Statistics estimates that roughly 97 percent of college graduates hit the labor market immediately after school. This is not necessarily surprising when you think that money is the main motive behind a college degree.

As I personally experienced, finding work after graduation doesn't always come easy. Although the amount of difficulty one faces while looking for a job varies from individual to individual, few people find pleasure in the process. For example, some people run into over qualification issues, others experience age discrimination, and some encounter a host of other issues relating to ethnicity, lack of experience, and so on.

There is yet another issue that is slowly developing that few college candidates anticipate prior to enrolling in school. Employers are continually becoming more selective because jobs are getting scarce. According to the Bureau of Labor Statistics, the projected job outlook for potential degree candidates between 1996 and 2006 will be less than anticipated. An average of 1.38 million applicants will be matched to approximately 1.13 million job openings each year, a projection of 250,000 annual jobs less than what's needed. In which case, only the most skilled and talented people will be considered first for job openings.

The Fading Value of the BS and BA Degrees

For most college attendees, a bachelor's degree is the highest college goal they'll ever attain. Roughly 73 percent of those who graduate with a baccalaureate degree choose to stay put. This move makes sense when you consider some of the following factors:

1. Since most people feel pressured to attend college, they're interested in doing only what's necessary to graduate.
2. Few people have the resources (time and money) to pursue a master's degree or anything higher.
3. The average income of an undergraduate is $45,678 per year—not too shabby for some people.

Unfortunately, for those who haven't noticed, the bachelors' degree is rapidly losing its value. These days, it appears that everybody has one, and in a competitive world, this situation speaks less favorable for those who hold BS or BA degrees. In fact, one could easily say that the market is saturated with undergraduate degrees, a condition that demotes the credential to the rank of a high school diploma.

Based on current trends, it is expected that those who don't have a college degree will eventually end up in a college or university sooner or later. The long-term implication is that when people submit a résumé to a company for a job, they'll be grouped with possibly thousands of applicants with the same credentials, making it harder for employers to spot good job candidates.

Jobseekers, especially those with a credential less than a master's degree, need to avoid becoming sedentary. Simply put, the law of supply and demand prevails here. The more prevalent the undergraduate degree becomes, the less attention it gets. Then those who hold the degree are faced with the choice of going back to school for a master's degree or risk losing their jobs.

The Master's Degree

The master's degree is still special. One of the reasons is because few people are able to attain it. Today, roughly 26 percent of college students feel motivated enough to pursue the degree. This number is likely to grow, however, because as the competition gets greater at the undergraduate level, more people will see the master's degree as an option to enhance their chances of getting ahead.

On the other hand, making the decision to pursue the master's degree should not be a haphazard choice, because in addition to spending a lot of money in the process of getting it, employers are now beginning to question its value. For example, research into forty years of data has provided little evidence that a master's degree actually improves one's career. Yet each year, the number of graduate-degree candidates grows. According to the National Center for Education Statistics, a total of 429,296 master's degrees were awarded in 1998 compared to 294,183 in 1981, a 46 percent increase in seven years.

Years ago, the assumption was that people who went to Harvard or Yale were fortunate. The salary earned after graduation would pay the cost of the MBA in a few short years. Those who went to other colleges or universities would be less likely to earn enough to pay the cost of their education.

Today, this concept carries less weight. Since there is an abundance of MBAs, employers are questioning the value of the education. They value, instead, connectivity, networking, and talent over an MBA. A recent study indicated that releasing 100,000 MBA graduates into the workforce each year does little to improve business value. The obsolete textbooks, static lectures, and outdated analyses have little comparison to the dynamic world of business. Therefore, today's companies are relying less and less on MBA graduates for up-to-date business strategies and leadership.

So while MBA hopefuls are looking at a bright financial future, the companies that hope to hire them have a different plan. They're looking for intelligent people with real-world experience. To them, this option holds more importance in a rapidly changing world than the MBA degree. So the extra two years invested for the MBA may not necessarily provide any extra benefit after all.

The School Debt

No matter how you look at it, the expense of achieving a college degree is not cheap. Though the costs include time, effort, and money, most people ignore the other two and focus on the money because that's what hurts the most. In Chapter 5, we quoted a $40,000 annual expense for attending private colleges in the United States. For all we know, this cost has far exceeded the means of an untold number of families in this country. Yet, there are indications that college fees will continue to rise. Some states have recently increased their college fees as high as 20 percent (the highest ever) for public colleges. Meanwhile, you can bet that private colleges and universities will also raise their fees.

Those who have college tuition paid by parents or by a company are fortunate. Most likely, these people will be walking away from campus owing nothing after graduation. Unfortunately, most college attendees don't have it this good. For them, borrowing money for tuition is the only means by which they can attend college. According to Sallie Mae, 61 percent of the nation's undergraduate students who attended a public college in school year 1999-2000 relied on loans. By the time they graduated, they owed an average of $16,000 in student loans. Moreover, 66 percent of those who attended nonprofit colleges relied on student loans to complete school. After graduation, this group owed an average of $18,900.

As with everything else, this trend is likely to continue far into the future. In the academic year 2001-2002, a little more 11 million loans were distributed to students and families. By 2009, the U.S. Department of Education expects the dollar amount of student loans to rise to $64 billion.

This vast amount of money says little about the real expense associated with the pursuit of a professional or master's degree, however. The cost per individual is astronomical. I personally left college owing the government roughly $75,000 in student loans. And based on conversations with fellow students, this amount is low in comparison to what they owe. Additionally, those who pursue professional degrees, such as doctors and lawyers, are leaving college with no less than $120,000 in student loans.

As bad as this may be, this is not the extent of the school debt. Adding to the student loan fiasco is the credit card problem. Eighty percent of all college students end up with credit card debts. In 2003, the average monthly credit card balance for undergraduates was $3,000 up from $1,879 in 1998. Of those who owed, 31 percent of them carried a balance of $7,000 according to one survey.

In light of this debt problem, most people who attend a four-year college or university have mixed emotions by the time they graduate. Their experience could be seen more like one of honey and vinegar. While they're generally happy that they've attained a college degree, the debt they created to pay for it becomes a long-term burden. Today, some college graduates are particularly concerned that they'll never be able to buy a house, raise children, and pay off their student loans as well as their other debts.

No doubt about it, this concern is legitimate. As mentioned in Chapter 5, the U.S. Department of Agriculture estimated that a family who earns $64,000 a year will spend roughly $16,000 a year to raise one child. If this is true, by the time the child reaches eighteen years old, the family will have spent a total of $288,000. Additionally, for every $5,000 debt balance, the probability of purchasing a house is reduced by 1 percent. This indicates that the more debt a person has, the less likely it is that the individual will own a home.

The problem gets worse. Six months after graduation, student loans come due by default. For most people, the thought of beginning to pay on that debt is a financial nightmare. They simply don't have the money to handle the responsibility. For this reason, Sallie Mae provides a forbearance option, allowing account holders to delay payments up to twelve months at a time. For millions of people around the country, including me, this option has become a salvation. It gives a person the opportunity to catch a breath, do some thinking, and develop a strategy to repay the debt.

Regrettably, the forbearance option itself becomes a trap. Each year one pushes the debt back, the loan accrues additional interest, ballooning the balance to an unbelievable amount. For instance, a $60,000 principal loan balance can quickly turn into a $100,000 loan mammoth five years later. This type situation discourages the most hopeful people among us. But for millions of students, the forbearance option is their only hope. But as they delay making payments on their student loans, one can only imagine the financial burden this will become as the debt gets larger.

A Degree of Justification

In a perfect world, success should beget success. In other words, as people increase their knowledge, experience, and credentials, they should also have a corresponding increase in pay or salary. But that's not always the case. In the real world, some people who are less qualified get better jobs and make more money. "Life is not fair," we all say.

But let's assume that all college graduates leave campus and walk directly into perfect working conditions. The first year on the job, they generate $100,000, five years later $200,000, and ten years later

$300,000. In that case, one could easily think that life would be bliss. Or would it?

Based on current behavioral trends, these individuals would still struggle financially. Today, regardless of our income level, we spend 100 percent of our take-home pay on house payments, utilities, cars, student loans, credit cards, furniture, and electronic equipment. That's up from 76 percent in 1992. In other words, each month, the majority of us spend all the money we make and then some—regardless of our income. When the cash is depleted, we simply borrow on credit cards to pay for the rest of our *wants*.

The Beneficiaries of Your College Degree

If you're like most people, the main reason for going to college is to improve your personal circumstance—no one else's. You want to be smarter so you can sell part of your talent, ability, and knowledge to a company that will pay you the equivalence in dollars. In return, you intend to use the money to pay for comfort, safety, health, protection, and financial security—the things we all want, and the more the better.

Again, assume that everything works out the way the culture predicts it. You have your degree, and it appears that you found the perfect career. It also appears that you're making a lot of money, and you have the prestige to go along with your lifestyle. If, after all your investment and hard work, you find yourself struggling from paycheck to paycheck, are you better off than before going to college?

I think not. If you have more debt than you had prior to earning the college degree, you're worse off now. Initially, you may not think so because your status could be getting in the way. But what's the value of your net worth? Is it where you expected it to be, or is it getting more negative by the year?

While you're pondering this thought, keep in mind that income, regardless how large, has little to do with wealth. In other words, If you're bringing in $300,000 a year and keeping little or none of it for yourself, you're broke. Worse, if you have debt and can't live without borrowing additional money to make ends meet, you're broke.

With these conditions, are you less stressed, more comfortable, safer, and more secure than prior to your college degree? My guess is that you're not. Instead, you're probably nervous and frustrated about your financial situation. And if you're not, you should be, because your debt poses a great threat to your long-term financial security.

If you haven't benefited in ways that you expected as a result of your college degree, could it be that others are profiting more from your investment? They would be (a) the college or university that received thousands and thousand of dollars from you for books and tuition; (b) the company that profits from your skills, knowledge, and abilities; (c) the government that collects more taxes on your higher salary; (d) the person or entity that collects interest payments from your student loans; or (e) all of the above.

If these possibilities are true, I think you get the message. It seems that every one gets a piece of your income while you struggle to make ends meet.

Meanwhile, you're wondering why you haven't achieved financial independence. Your circumstances have been close to being perfect: you are well-educated; you have your college degrees; you have a good paying job; you've worked long and hard for roughly 20 years; and you've made a lot of money during those years. What happened?

Recommendations for Those Who Planning to Attend a College or University

If you already have a college degree, I want to personally congratulate you for making the effort to earn one. My hope is that your life has improved because of it. On the other hand, if you're like most college graduates, the credential hasn't made one bit of difference in your financial life other than increasing your debt load.

If you are contemplating pursuing a college degree, you need to consider the following:

a. This move will most likely plunge you into serious debt. That means that after graduation, you won't be starting your financial equation at zero but below zero. At that level, it will take you years to break even, if ever.

b. There is no guarantee that you'll receive a raise, promotion, or new job. In fact, your income may not change at all.

c. No one owes you anything just because you've earned a college degree. Furthermore, remember that "no one cares about it." Take this part to heart because it's true.

At the same time, it's wise to focus on some of the following suggestions. If you do, chances are, you won't be disappointed:

a. Plan to expand your knowledge and personal development, e.g., more intelligence, self-esteem, personal fulfillment.
b. Become a role model for your children by being an inspiration, challenging them to pursue a higher education.
c. Expect your degree to earn you an interview, but not necessarily a job or financial independence.

CHAPTER 9

Autoculture Jobs

(Cultural Trap No. 4)

Years ago, occupational choices were limited to only farming,construction, and coal mining. As late as 1979, the aspiring job in the country was the ultimate front desk clerk position. Prior to that period, people were happy to be laborers, carpenters, ditch diggers, auto mechanics, phone operators, and farmers.

Today, our job choices have evolved into an unlimited number of options. For instance, one could be an engineer, nurse, computer programmer, news reporter, teacher, accountant, advertiser, salesperson, real-estate agent, police officer, and so forth.

Essentially, job diversity is an integral component of every healthy economy. Not only does it boost the gross national product but it also creates occupational choices, something Americans have grown to love. Today, the work choice of even the fussiest individual can be satisfied. One has the opportunity to follow literally any path to achieve financial prosperity.

But as convenient as this is, the variety-pack job market has its drawbacks. It has caused us to be highly selective when looking for work so much so that we've become occupationally biased. Over the years, we have intuitively developed two main job groupings: *good* and *bad*. A job is good if we like the package the employer offers. Conversely, if we don't like the job package, the job is bad.

No one wants a bad job. It's usually laden with restrictions and undesirable conditions that most of us have grown to dislike: bad bosses, low pay, long hours, etc. As a result, we take as much time as possible to find what we consider to be a good job. You've heard the comments, "I'm looking for a good job," or "I haven't found a good job," etc.

Is there such a thing as a good job? Could it be that the culture has staged an occupational condition to create an acceptable standard in our minds? Could it be that we've simply grown to accept a situation that the majority of Americans believe to be good or suitable?

Job Satisfaction

There is no question that some people love their jobs. They like the company, the tasks they perform, the work environment, the salary, and the benefits. A survey of 5,000 U.S. workers conducted in 2000 indicated that 50.7 percent of people were satisfied with their jobs, a 13.8 percent drop when compared to 58.6 percent of respondents who were asked the same question in 1995.

When we look at the other side of the same survey, we see that a little less than half of the America's workforce is either dissatisfied or somewhat dissatisfied with their jobs. One can only assume that these workers ended up with what the culture has labeled a *bad* job.

The question is, what causes some people to like their jobs while others dislike them? Could it be that some people fall in love with the company they work for e.g. company's culture, work environment, boss, supervisor, etc? Could it be the type of work that they do? Or does it have to do largely with the pay and benefits they receive on the job? As you can see, there are many variables to consider when distinguishing the difference between good and bad jobs.

Yet for most Americans, the deductive reasoning is simple. Though the foregoing benefits are important, we decide whether a job is good or bad based on the company's perks. Studies show that we enjoy the work environment when the perks are plenty. We brag and make positive comments about the companies that provide them. Consequently, in addition to the traditional benefits such as medical, dental, retirement plans, promotional opportunities, and so on, some large companies go all out to provide one or more fringe benefits to make their employees happy. Some of the best known perks are listed below:

- Yoga classes
- Family rooms
- Volleyball and basketball courts
- Softball fields
- Chair massagers and locker-room showers
- Welcome breakfasts

- Job rotations
- Friday-night beer bashes
- Free medical and dental services from on-site clinics
- On-site child care at half cost
- Generous profit sharing and stock options
- Awards for selfless behaviors
- Free dinners for those who work late
- Easter egg hunts and Valentine's Day cookies
- Regular potlucks
- Free Thanksgiving turkeys
- Paid memberships in an off-site gym

In a broad sense, we've come to expect American companies to provide the traditional benefits—medical, dental, retirement plans, etc. Most do. So, the tie breaker comes down to perks. And the companies that provide the most of them are the winners—the good jobs. Others are classified as bad ones.

This is all well and good. One should take advantage of all the security, comfort, and convenience that's available from the employer. On the other, keep in mind that the "good job" criteria are conditional. In other words, the perks and benefits won't last forever. The big salary, the fabulous office, the great retirement plan, and all the other fringe benefits will last only as long as the company can afford them.

In the event that things get tough, companies retain the right to make changes within their establishments. In which case, some of the first things to disappear are the perks, leaving those who depend on them reevaluating their contributions to those companies.

Today, more American workers are getting disappointed about jobs that they once considered "good." Their lives have been turned upside down too many times as a result of, so called, bad employers' decisions. A December 2003 survey found that 80 percent of employees are dissatisfied with their jobs. Sixty percent of those surveyed said that they're stressed and overworked. Fifty-six percent claimed that they're dissatisfied with current perks and benefits.

For those who are familiar with the nature of a job, none of this is surprising. By virtue of the fact that they've hopped around from employment to employment, they've come to realize that one should expect nothing more from a job than a salary. For that matter, they've concluded that the only "good jobs" out there are the ones that haven't been found because once they've been discovered, all of their skeletons begin to show in a matter of months. Consequently, the only ones left to be surprised are people who still believe in the so-called "good job" concept. It's only a matter of time before they realize that such a thing doesn't exist.

The Attributes of a Job

If you're an inexperienced job seeker, much of this information could be hard to swallow, especially if you have a college degree and see a clear path to success through a job.

Nevertheless, the day you get hired by a company, you need to understand one major point regarding your job. And that is, as long as you remain employed by that company, you place your economic situations at risk. In other words, the day you walk into the office, sit down at your desk, and start feeling comfortable, you've compromised your economic position to lose. Realistically, you could be the most brilliant thinker, planner, and organizer in your field of work. As a result, you may have the tendency to feel indispensable. But no matter how good you are, you can be replaced at any time.

Control through Separation

The thing that every employee needs to keep in mind is that within the context of a job, (e.g., the task performed, the steady income, the pension plan, the medical and dental benefits, the paid vacations, all the perks, and so forth) lies a very subtle but effective message. The condition is, management retains control over everything. This concept is undisputed and comes within the same initial job package or offer received.

One of the clear signs of management control is through *separation*. As an employee, you're considered an outsider, meaning, regardless how gifted you are, your duties will be limited to a defined set of responsibilities, thereby restricting your movement within the company. The main reason is because the internal affairs of the operation are sensitive and are reserved for a privileged few unless, of course, you hold a critical position such as chief executive officer, chief financial officer, or owner. These individuals are considered insiders with access to information otherwise kept from the regular employees.

For most workers, this is not a bother. In fact, some people like the separation between employees and management. It allows them the chance to be physically detached from the company. At the same time, most workers develop emotional ties with their companies. This is especially true for those who are content with their salaries and benefits. Consequently, it's not unusual to hear people refer to their work as "my job, my company," and so forth. These employees obviously feel a sense of connection to the company even though they may not be stakeholders.

This sense of vicarious ownership or connectivity is not entirely deceptive. In fact, it's quite healthy for employees to identify with a well-established company. Such a relationship provides people a sense of self-worth, dignity, and purpose. At the same time, these employees benefit the companies they work for by being more productive, committed, and loyal.

However, caution is needed here because it is within this type of relationship that most employees get blindsided. Given the fact that few employees know about a company's internal affairs, most of them never know what's being planned until it's too late. For instance, management could be drafting plans for layoffs, bankruptcy, etc.—decisions that could adversely affect employees—yet the information could be withheld from them until the last minute. When these events occur, those who are affected the most are employees who are most loyal and committed to the company.

Control through Salary

Everyone would like the opportunity to earn more money. Since it provides the means by which we do just about everything, the more of it we have, the better we feel. As such, most of us remain hopeful that that as we continue to work, we'll generate more income to improve our lifestyle. Unfortunately, most people don't realize that they'll never be able to make the kind of money they expect by working for someone else.

If this concept is foreign to you, consider the following: In our world of varied occupations, every service has a price, most of which is established by the company that hired you. Therefore, it's an employer's responsibility to measure your income by paying you the value of your service. So while you may be dreaming of major purchases and extensive vacations, you may not realize that the company you work for has imposed a *salary cap* on your income.

Remember, the company is not in business to cheat you of your salary. Realistically, it will pay you the going rate based on the service you provide. So in some ways, it is the economy itself that imposes the rate on your income, and your employer is simply following the guidelines.

At first, the *salary cap* may not seem to be a problem. In fact, most people are satisfied with a company's initial offer unless it's outrageously low, and there is no chance of having an increase. A *salary cap* is not a small issue. It literally limits your potential for making additional money when you need it. For that reason, when your income is limited, so is your lifestyle.

Sure, at each job anniversary, you may get a 3 percent to 5 percent cost of living increase in your salary. But how many people do you see get rich by simply keeping up with inflation? It doesn't take long to realize that each raise is quickly consumed by taxes before it gets to you. And by the time the remaining portion is seen on your paycheck, you're desperately in need of another raise. As you continue working for the same company, you eventually come to realize that you're making no financial progress.

Should you blame your employer for this problem? Some people do. If you're unhappy with your income predicament, you should blame no one but yourself. It was you who placed yourself in that position. Since you accepted the company's offer, you also accepted the *salary cap.*

What you may not realize is that as long as you subject yourself to the *salary cap,* you will continue to experience financial hardship. Here is why: while your income remains flat, your *needs* and *wants* never stop growing. What is more is that prices of goods and services always increase as a result of inflation, expanding your expenses each month. Meantime, your employer remains insensitive to your personal needs and refuses to compromise by raising your salary. So you continue doing the best you can until you get a promotion or find another job. Then, the cycle starts all over again.

Control through Layoffs

If you've worked in this country long enough and haven't experienced the inconvenience of being fired from a job, consider yourself lucky. My guess is that you've heard about the horrifying experiences some people go through as a result of losing their jobs.

As an employee, you shouldn't uncross your fingers, because as long as you continue working for someone else, the threat remains real. Every day, the newspapers and televisions tell us about recent and anticipated layoffs. Seemingly, employers from every industry have been letting people go by the thousands. And while those who still have a job continue to pray, hoping to avert the threat, companies continue to announce more layoffs.

Nothing is more powerful in a company's management arsenal than the layoff option. More than the ability to control a person's *freedom* and *salary,* management can terminate an individual's employment at will. As a result, this action is the most revered punishment an employee can experience. The decision is usually quick, unexpected, and permanent, leaving the employee strapped. As such, the one who initiates the action is usually seen as cold, inconsiderate, and brutal.

But blaming a company for exercising a layoff option is not necessarily the best response under the circumstances. This type of behavior is usually unproductive because it does little to change management decisions. Frankly, dismissals are ways of safeguarding a company's interests. And although the action may appear to be unreasonable to an outsider, this option has always been a part of the job agreement from the beginning.

Understandably, management is not responsible for the financial or emotional outcome of employees during a dismissal. Victims of layoffs are usually left to fend for themselves while companies do what they must to stay competitive.

The Downsizing

These days, a lot of layoffs are being blamed on downsizing, a condition by which management exercises a forced reduction to cut costs. Usually, the need is stimulated by various economic conditions such as low revenue, amalgamation, change in company's mission, change in management policy, and so forth.

For the most part, downsizing makes sense, but only to management. From its point of view, the action is absolutely necessary to prevent the company from filing Chapter 11 bankruptcy or folding altogether. Most employees, on the other hand, don't see it that way. Those who are to be laid off see the whole thing as punishment that they don't deserve, especially when they had little to do with the problem. Yet their jobs are being sacrificed to cure a problem that management may have mislabeled. As a result, some people walk away feeling cheated and resentful.

Years ago, employee layoffs were less common mainly because economic conditions were more stable, making it less likely for people to move from job to job. Consequently, some people worked as long as thirty or forty years for the same company until they retired.

Times have changed, however. Today, economic conditions have become more elusive. Therefore, companies are being forced to continually assess and reassess their positions in order to remain competitive in a global market. Accordingly, management is sometimes faced with the unfortunate task of laying off thousands of people in order to keep their companies afloat. The resulting impact, of course, is that millions of people are suddenly pushed into the unemployment line unexpectedly. There, they receive a small weekly paycheck that barely comes close to making ends meet. But the unemployment check becomes a lifesaver in desperate moments such as this. Though the money is small, it serves as a bridge to the next job or career.

Unemployment is nothing new. Neither has it ended. Figure 9.1 shows a trend for the last thirteen years. Notice that although the numbers have changed slightly from year to year between 1989 and 2002, the rates have stayed consistent at an average of 5.5 percent (see figure 9.1).

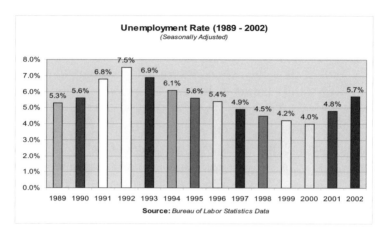

Unemployment Rate (1989 - 2002)
(Seasonally Adjusted)

Source: *Bureau of Labor Statistics Data*

Fig. 9.1

At a time when downsizing is common, a 5.5 percent unemployment rate may not appear to be consequential. But don't underestimate this small number. For example, a 4.8 percent unemployment rate in 2001 represented 6.7 million Americans out of work, people who once had paychecks but found themselves without a job.

The unsettling feeling is knowing that unemployment is far from being over. On August 5, 2003, the Bureau of Labor Statistics reported that the unemployment rate was 6.1 percent. The report indicated that 93,000 nonfarm jobs were lost, 431,000 manufacturing jobs vanished, and 212,000 communication jobs dissipated.

As recently as June 8, 2005, General Motors (GM) announced laying off 25,000 blue-collar jobs and closing down several U.S. plants in the next four years as it struggles to bring production up to par with sales. The company also announced cutting back expensive healthcare benefits for workers and risked an argument with its union.

This decision affects more than GM workers. Steel plants and other main GM suppliers will also feel the impact. Many of them will be forced to cut back production, creating an inevitable layoff.

This is by no means the end of this type of development. Layoffs will continue as long as market conditions remain unpredictable. When companies are backed up against the wall as a result of negatively marketing situations, employees are generally the first to go. Therefore, since we have no idea when a downsizing will occur, the operating word for all employees is *caution*.

The Age Alert

For all we know, employees get laid off for quantifiable reasons such as downsizing, amalgamation, going out of business, etc. Furthermore, people get fired for objectionable issues such as poor performance, noncompliance, repeated tardiness, and so forth. Never will a company admit to laying off a person because of age. Yet it happens every day.

As it stands, American companies are becoming less and less tolerant with older workers. Some CEOs believe that an individual's productivity peaks around forty-three years old. And so, many older workers are being pushed away from jobs for no reason.

This type of thing generally happens at the worse time in people's lives, a time when most Americans are getting serious about retirement planning. But unfortunately, this situation has little to do with management.

Nonetheless, more and more American workers are being faced with this embarrassing situation. My own wife, for example, became a victim of this stealth conduct. After spending seven successful years working for a well-established corporation, she woke up one day and realized that she was a candidate for dismissal. She, a model worker with flawless reputation in both her personal and professional life, was stunned.

What she didn't know was that management had other plans for her. Since the company was merging, it was instructed to reduce its workforce. Thus, at forty-five years old, my wife was suddenly unable to please her bosses, regardless how hard she tried. The harder she worked to please them, the more incompatible she became with the company's new culture.

In the last two years with the company, she was nothing less than a ball of nerves as she tried to keep her job. Management literally put her through hell, trying to force her out of the company for no reason at all. After two years of continual harassment, she decided to walk away with a small severance package. Her position was then filled by a younger employee who cost the company much less in salary and benefits.

Another striking example is the case of a forty-five year old man who, again, woke up one day and realized that his job was given to a twenty-eight year old male. He, after receiving a letter of dismissal from his company, sat in a chair and read it eight times. "I couldn't believe it," he said, after absorbing the information. The news struck him so hard that it felt like someone had hit him in his stomach.

Another gentleman had invested the last twenty-seven years of his life in this company. He started there at age twenty-one and had decided to stay put until retirement. On June 6, 1998, he was one of 390 employees who received a letter of dismissal. Seventy percent of those who got laid off were past forty.

Numerous studies have shown that older workers bring more value to a company than younger ones. The reasons are obvious: older workers are more knowledgeable, loyal, and committed to a company's mission. They exercise better judgment, and they are less likely to quit when things get difficult and uncomfortable.

Some companies remain biased in favor of younger workers. For those companies, younger workers add spice to the work environment. They are more adaptable to change and more flexible when learning new skills, particularly in a global market where technology reigns supreme. Consequently, younger workers have become good candidates for innovative companies.

In the not so distant future, many people see companies becoming more tolerant and, in some cases, desperately needing older American workers. The low birth rate in the past four decades will create a huge shortage in the work force. As a result, the Baby Boomer generation will once again be in high demand in the job market. But this forecast does little to assuage the pain of those who are currently feeling the brunt of management reprisal in respect to aging workers. Seeing their jobs being taken and turned over to workers who are young enough to be their sons and daughters is not only embarrassing, but also nerve-racking.

The younger workers, on the other hand, are capitalizing on the same trend that puts their parents out of work. It provides them the opportunity to skyrocket their careers in the corporate world at a young age. Also, it gives them a chance to prove their leadership abilities over someone who is much older.

But younger people who take pleasure in replacing older workers on the job should remain cautious as well. Ethically, the act of capitalizing on someone else's physiological disadvantage is morally questionable. But more so, it won't be long before they find themselves in the same predicament as their parents. That's the nature of a job.

The High-Salary Threat

Employees who escape the wrath of management layoffs through *downsizing* or *aging* are not out of the woods yet. Along with so many other things that can go wrong on a work site, eventually leading to an employee dismissal, the *salary threat* remains a big problem. Management is getting more and more cautious of people who draw high salaries from payroll. They're finding it difficult to justify the return in production. What they see, instead, are high-salaried employees who are depleting the company's profits. For example, a sales executive who earned $132,000 annually felt pretty secure on his job until he was suddenly replaced by a younger worker who was happy to do the work for less.

There was a computer engineer who invested fourteen years of her life in a company. She generated $180,000 in annual salary and hoped to retire from the company. She was suddenly replaced by someone who was willing to do the work for less pay. At forty-four years old, she had no income and was forced to find employment elsewhere. The sad thing was, more than the inconvenience of finding another job, she could expect to make no more than half of her previous salary, an income that would barely cover her current financial obligations.

For what it's worth, the high-salary threat is not targeted towards a few people. Anyone who draws heavy on company's payroll is at risk of getting replaced or having a pay cut. For some employers, the plan is simple. For $40,000 or $50,000 a year, management can take graduates from college, train them, give them long-term options, and own them. These employees will do exactly what management wants, and if they don't, they'll get fired.

The choices are not that simple with older workers. According to management, they draw two or three times more salary than younger ones, have more bad working habits, don't care to listen to supervisors, and do half the work.

Deductively, forty year old employees with large salaries are under management scrutiny. And in today's economic climate, these two components *(age* and *high salaries)* make a deadly combination in respect to one's long-term career.

A Job Is a Job, Is a Job

No question about it, a job without the threat of layoffs and income limitations would make an ideal economic solution for millions of people. Not only would it provide a continuous flow of graduating income, but it would also eliminate a lot of economic fears such as repossessions, foreclosures, and bankruptcies.

Of course, this type of expectation is unrealistic because our economic system isn't designed that way. Instead, what we've come to realize is that there is no such thing as a "good job" in America. Regardless of how appealing a job may appear to be at first, the characteristics are the same—a job will always be a job. That means, the working environment may be safe, friendly, and comfortable; the supervisors and bosses may appear to be friendly; the salary, benefits, and perks may be fabulous. But the nature of the job never changes. The risk of getting laid off always exists and could be triggered by many factors, most of which have been mentioned.

We've all heard about people who've lost their jobs for one reason or another. What we don't get to see are the human lives that are impacted by the loss. We assume that those who get pink slips will quickly find another job to replace their income. But that's not always the case. Some people struggle for months and even years before finding another job. According to the Center for Policy Research, workers who were laid off between 1990 and 1992, 40 percent of them were still unemployed two years later. And those who had an income of roughly $23,000 a year watched their salary dwindle to a meager $12,000.

That's not the worst of it. When people lose their only source of income, their whole way of life changes. In addition to possibly going hungry, various debt obligations fall behind. Until they find another way to generate income, they're left wide open for creditors' harassment.

Unfortunately, many people end up losing their possessions. Their homes, automobiles, and other valuables are, sometimes, repossessed, making life even more difficult while looking for another job. Lately, according to the Mortgage Bankers Association of America, foreclosure rates have reached a thirty-year high. In a three-month period ending in June 2003, lenders initiated 134,886 new foreclosure notices. And while foreclosure rates on Federal Housing Administration (FHA) financed loans have increased by 37 percent recently, foreclosures on conventional loans have risen up to 45 percent, an eleven-year high.

Adding to the home foreclosure reality is bankruptcy. When people see the writing on the wall, they usually try to file for bankruptcy to avert foreclosures on their homes. However, this option is plagued with its own economic woes. Those who file bankruptcy usually face credit denial and high interest rate problems in the future. Nonetheless, millions of people use bankruptcy as a solution when things get too tough. As of December 31, 2004, over 2.0 million Americans had filed personal bankruptcy compared to 1.6 in September 30, 2003.

Yet, none of these statistics show the emotional impact on families experiencing these problems. One can only imagine the emotional stress accompanying them. It's simply impossible to stay emotionally and psychologically composed while watching your lifestyle evaporate right before your eyes. Although some people handle these problems differently, one would be more or less than human to *not* feel helpless and confused.

When bad things happen to us, we have a tendency to blame others. We look for scapegoats wherever we can find them. Some of us blame the bank or lien holder for a repossession, foreclosure, or bankruptcy; some people blame their previous employers in the case of a layoff; some of us blame the economy; yet others blame everything on the president of the United States.

Meanwhile, few of us see a problem associated with our dependency on other people to employ us. Instead of finding ways to generate our own income, we've come to expect others to provide it. When they can't continue to supply the salary, benefits, and perks we expect, we feel slighted.

Recommendations for Job Seekers

Jobs are, unquestionably, essential components to our way of life. Companies need employees that are able to provide competitive skills in a competitive market. Those who are looking for work need to know that they can sell their services for a competitive salary. These situations create a mutual arrangement for both parties.

However, each employee needs to keep in mind the dispensability factors associated with a job. Therefore, it's important that each employee treat a job only as a temporary income arrangement. Any long-term expectation or job dependency will, undoubtedly, disappoint the worker in the end.

The solution, of course, is to develop multiple streams of income, thereby stabilizing one's personal economic situation on a long-term basis.

CHAPTER 10

Autoculture Taxation

(Cultural Trap No. 5)

By and large, the risk associated with being employed by someone else is not necessarily the biggest obstacle to building personal wealth. Job limitations such as salary caps and layoffs can be controlled to some degree with good planning. Therefore, assuming you're able to overcome many of the employment handicaps, there is yet another major obstacle to personal wealth-building that you need to overcome. That impediment is government taxation.

Initially, this concept may not be easy to grasp because so many people are blinded to the punitive nature of taxes. They're naive enough to think that the government couldn't possibly stand in their way to financial independence. But think of it this way. What is the greatest incentive for waking up each morning and going to work? The need for money, of course. Certainly, the job provides additional benefits such as the meaningful interactions with coworkers, the satisfaction of making a contribution to society, and the sense of personal dignity, knowing that you're earning your own wages. Yet all of these are by-products of the main reason for working. At the end of an exhaustive day, week, or month, the thing that matters the most is the paycheck.

The interesting thing is that as badly as you need your money, the government depends on it just as much. Therefore, as you plan to use your income to provide for your family, Uncle Sam is continually scheming to take as much from it as possible to conduct business. So one could imagine a fight between you and the government, the purpose of which is to determine who gets to keep the most from your paycheck.

For you, the struggle isn't easy because the government is crafty and determined. As lawmakers manipulate the tax laws, their goal is to hide the truth from you, making it difficult to know how much tax you pay on a regular basis. As a result, you may be shocked to realize how much of your money goes to paying taxes each year. And when you come to grips with the reality, you'll see that nothing in our culture is more adversely affecting your financial progress than taxes.

According to the Tax Foundation, Americans worked from January 1 through April 11, 2004, to pay their tax obligations to the government. Roughly four months of your income was taken from you last year for taxes.

The interesting thing is, if all of this money were to be taken from you at the same time, you'd be screaming "murder." And Uncle Sam knows that. Besides, if lawmakers left you with no money to keep you and your family alive for four months, how could the government collect future taxes from you? You would be starving, sick, or dead during those months. Instead, the same portion of money is taken from you incrementally to avert a sudden negative impact on your lifestyle. Also, this gradual peeling away money from you each month is a method the government prefers in order to hide its real motive.

In the remaining portion of this chapter, we'll peek into the government taxation scheme to see how most of us are being manipulated by taxes. It's interesting to note that in the past ten years, we've spent more days working to pay taxes than any other household items on the budget. For example, according to the chart below, tax working days have jumped to 117 days compared to 106 days for shelter, food, and clothing combined (see figure 10.1).

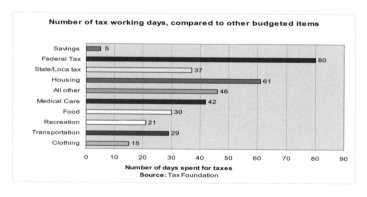

Fig. 10.1

But taxes on personal income is nothing new. The concept has been around since 1861 when it became necessary to raise money for the American Civil War. Back then, the tax rate was 3 percent on $800 a year, exempting the majority of wage earners. Then, in 1862, the tax rate was raised to 5 percent on income over $10,000 a year, broadening the tax base.

After the war, the public became concerned about ongoing taxation. The pervading attitude among the people was "no war, no taxes." Suddenly, taxation without a cause appeared unethical and a direct violation on personal freedom. Yet Congress chose to ignore the public and continued collecting taxes without justification.

Meanwhile, the government kept spending more money each year, making it difficult to balance the budget with revenue from tariffs alone. In 1893, Congress passed laws making income tax a primary target to help balance the budget.

In 1895, the Supreme Court ruled that the practice of taxation on personal income was unconstitutional, forcing Congress to rethink its tax strategy. Meanwhile, the president of the United States (William Howard Taft) introduced the Sixteenth Amendment, making tax on personal income a constitutional issue. In 1913, the practice of taxation became legally binding.

Since then, Congress has become extremely creative with the tax laws. Lawmakers have conveniently found ways to either raise the tax rate or create new laws whenever the budget goes out of control. For instance, during World War II, federal spending skyrocketed to $95 billion in 1945 up from $9.6 billion in 1940. Within that period, the tax rates were between 19 percent on $2,000 and 88 percent on $200,000, spreading the tax base from 14 million to 50 million taxpayers.

But the changes didn't stop there. Since 1943, Congress has made approximately thirty different revisions to the tax laws, many of which lasted no more than a year before the next change. The tax evolution continued until 2001 when lawmakers decided to create six tax brackets and lower the rates slightly. Up until then, between 1993 and 2001, the tax rates were divided into five brackets, and they remained that way for approximately eight years, the longest stable tax period in American history (see table 10.1).

Table 10.1 (Tax Rates and Filing Status)					
% of tax rate	15%	28%	31%	36%	39.6%
Filing Status					
Single	$26,250	$63,550	$231,600	$288,350	Over $288,350
Head of house	$35,150	$90,800	$147,050	$288,350	Over $288,350
Married filing Jntly	$43,850	$105,950	$161,450	$288,350	Over $288,350
Married filing Sep.	$21,925	$52,975	$80,725	$144,175	Over $144,175

At this point, the obvious question is, why has Congress found it necessary to change the tax laws so frequently? The answer is simple. Since government continually overspends, lawmakers are continually trying to find ways to generate additional revenue. For example, in 1990, the federal government received $1 trillion in tax revenue and spent $1.3 trillion. This pattern has been pretty consistent over the years, making it difficult to stay within budget.

Unfortunately, whenever this type of situation occurs, personal income becomes the main target for additional revenue.

Direct Taxation

The direct tax is somewhat simple. It's the portion of money that's taken out of your income before you get your paycheck. This portion of money goes to pay for things such as state and federal taxes, Medicare, Social Security, and so forth. To determine how much tax an employee pays, each one of us is placed in a tax bracket based on level of income. For instance, prior to the Tax Relief Act of 2001, the tax rates reflected 15 percent, 28 percent, 31 percent, 36 percent, and 39.6 percent (see table 10.2). The higher the income, the higher the tax rate. Fortunately, most American taxpayers fell within the 15 percent tax bracket.

Interestingly enough, income tax is not the only source of government revenue. Our state and federal governments collect corporate income tax, excise tax, estate tax, gift tax, capital gains tax, and more. Yet taxes on individual income make up roughly 52 percent of government revenue.

This is not surprising when you consider the amount of money each working American pays in taxes. And this is the point. Because only a few of us pay attention to the various ways we pay taxes, the government continues to sap more and more of our income, leaving us with less and less money to spend for personal needs. Again, prior to the 2001 Tax Relief Act, the amount of money you paid in taxes may be larger than what you think simply because you haven't taken the time to look at the whole picture. Here is a breakdown:

For the moment, disregard your filing status and assume that you paid income tax based on the 15 percent tax bracket, in which case, you probably paid the government closer to 30 percent of your income in *direct taxes* (see table 10.2).

Table 10.2 (The Direct Tax)					
The Direct tax on income	15% Tax Brckt	28% Tax Brckt	31% Tax Brckt)	36% Tax Brckt	39.6% Tax Brckt
Federal tax rate	15	28	31	36	39.6
Social Security	6.2	6.2	6.2	6.2	6.2
Medicare	1.45	1.45	1.45	1.45	1.45
Average State tax (income)	6.47	6.47	6.47	6.47	6.47
Total Tax	29.27%	42.4%	45.12%	50.48%	54.12%

You may not have realized that you paid this much tax on your income because of the various fragmented sections of the tax laws and the method by which taxes are collected. But as you look back on the situation, you had roughly 70 percent of your income at your disposal for basic necessities, leaving you with little or no financial flexibility in the end. In other words, the dollar can be stretched only so far. The more of it the government takes, the less of it you get to keep.

Indirect Taxation

Having expended 30 percent of your income in taxes, one would think you've paid more than your fair share. But this amount doesn't reflect your total tax contribution for the given year. Whether you realized it or not, the remaining 70 percent of your income (the take-home portion) was subjected to additional state and local taxes as well.

As you conducted business, you continued paying taxes without even thinking about it. The reason is because these taxes are well hidden within the normal flow of day-to-day business. And because you don't see them, they don't bother you. For example, you paid taxes on the automobile you purchased, the gasoline in the tank, the clothes you wear, some of the food you eat, and on various other items. Much of these, of course, went unnoticed.

This type of taxation is generally referred to as *sales tax.* But more appropriately, the name should be called *back-end taxation.* It's a state and local government way of reaching into your back pocket without guilt or remorse, depleting your financial resources surreptitiously. The whole idea is that you'll pay the taxes without knowing the difference. And the method works very effectively.

If you are buying a house, the property tax is also included as an *indirect tax* because this portion of money is part of your disposable income. And although it's paid annually, a portion of it is usually deposited into an impound account through your mortgage payments.

Altogether, as we reassess your tax situation, you paid closer to 35 percent of your income in *direct* and *indirect* taxes, leaving you with approximately $0.65 on each dollar to buy the things you need to survive (see table 10.3).

Table 10.3 (The Direct & Indirect Tax)					
The Direct tax on income	**15% Tax Brckt**	**28% Tax Brckt**	**31% Tax Brckt**	**36% Tax Brckt**	**39.6% Tax Brckt**
Federal tax rate	15	28	31	36	39.6
Social Security	6.2	6.2	6.2	6.2	6.2
Medicare	1.45	1.45	1.45	1.45	1.45
Average State tax (income)	6.47	6.47	6.47	6.47	6.47
The Indirect tax					
Average Sales tax (US Avrg)	6.18	6.18	6.18	6.18	6.18
Average Property Tax rate Per ($100)	2.21%	2.21%	2.21%	2.21%	2.21%
Total Tax	*35.5%*	*48.6%*	*51.3%*	*56.7%*	*60.3%*

Taxpayers who were in the 39.6 percent tax bracket had it worse. They paid roughly $0.60 on each dollar, leaving them with $0.40 for spending.

Until now, you may have never seen or understood the implication of taxation in this fashion. And that's one of the major disadvantages with the system. Because the language is so complicated, the average American has given up trying to understand it. Consequently, it's hard to measure the day-to-day impact on personal income. Worse, most of us have gotten complacent in regard to taxation, making it even easier for lawmakers to continue fooling us with their tax schemes.

But this attitude is exactly what Congress was hoping to achieve. Over the years, they have deliberately manipulated the tax system to baffle the public. The concept is simple: if the general public remains confused about the system, the easier it will be to rob them. So while the majority of Americans assume that they are paying no more than 15 percent tax on their income, the actual amount is astonishingly higher. Hidden taxes, in the form of fees as well as the common income tax, are continually depleting our income. And as the government stays well supplied with revenue, the long-term tax implication on the individual is devastating.

Supposedly, the Tax Relief Act of 2001 has reduced the tax burden slightly. Between 2001 and 2006, the law promises to reduce the rates by half a point each year (see table 10.4).

Table 10.4 (Income Tax Rate Reduction of 2001)						
Tax Rates (Prior-2001)		15%	28%	31%	36%	39.6%
Tax Rates (2001-2006)	10%	15%	25%	28%	33%	35%
Filing status						
Single & Head of household	$221 to $808	$808 to $2,567	$2,567 to $5,708	$5,708 to $12,392	$12,392 to $26,767	$26,767 & Over
Married	$667 to $1,858	$1,858 to $5,396	$5,396 to $9,838	$9,838 to $15,463	$15,463 to $27,175	$27,175 & Over

Affirmatively, any reduction in the tax rate is a good thing. One less penny the government takes from us is one more penny in our pockets. But one penny at a time is hardly enough to create any major change in our lives. So if lawmakers are trying to show their generosity by reducing the tax rate, let it be something substantial.

Few people will recognize the difference on their paychecks in regard to the change in the Tax Relief Act of 2001. The margin is too small. At the end of the six-year period, the total average tax reduction will be roughly 3.4 percent.

To put this in perspective, most of us can relate to the 3 to 5 percent pay raise each year, the typical pay hike that most people come to expect in a good economy. But honestly, the annual raise is hardly enough to make a significant change in our lifestyle. One of the reasons is by the time the trickle-down portion gets to us, we barely notice the difference in our paychecks. Yet this is a situation where one has access to the entire 3 to 5 percent increase all at once.

The Tax Relief Act of 2001 will be fully implemented in 2006. Until then, most people will experience only half a point reduction in the tax rate each year, a change barely enough to see or make any difference in take-home pay. Also, should there be any increase in income as a result of this new law, state and local governments are waiting to hike their rates to gobble up the difference. So tell me, who's winning?

The bottom line is this: It makes no difference who collects the tax (federal, state, or local government) or for what purpose. The outcome is the same. Whether the tax is a *direct tax* on your income *(front-end taxation)* or an *indirect tax* when you shop *(back-end taxation)*, the money is being taken from you, making life more and more difficult.

Meanwhile, if you're unable to achieve your financial dream as a result of excessive tax, do you think Congress cares about you personally? I like to think that lawmakers have more important things on their minds than to be concerned about individual Americans who are homeless, hungry, and broke.

If you think that I'm opposed to paying taxes, your assumption would be incorrect. I file my taxes each year, and I owe the government nothing in back taxes.

However, the rationale is not whether one should or shouldn't pay taxes. I personally believe that our federal, state, and local governments need a certain amount of money to perform essential functions of government. We need the military, the National Guard, roads and highways, national security, research, and any other functions of government deemed necessary to protect the citizens of this country. Nevertheless, I'm opposed to paying taxes for inflated government spending, particularly senseless programs used for political advantages.

Frankly, it's not fun watching 30 to 40 percent of your income go into taxes, especially if you're struggling to make ends meet and can't save a dime. The worse part of it is to realize that most of that money gets squandered on political frivolity while you stay broke. Yet the government doesn't seem to understand why you can't save.

In some ways, little can be done with the way things are. Too many Americans have come to depend on government pork-belly spending—programs that do little good for anybody. However, the next time a politician talks to you about raising taxes, you ought to be concerned because while the cause may be right, and you don't mind making an additional financial contribution, you'll ultimately be hurting yourself. Whatever you do, keep in mind that every additional penny you allow to be taken from you is one less penny you have to feed your family and to improve your personal circumstances.

CHAPTER 11

Autoculture Credit and Debt

(Cultural Trap No. 6)

We, Americans, use credit to complete most of our business transactions. One of the main reasons is the accessibility of credit. But as convenient as this tool has become in our personal and professional lives, credit is another economic trap that's preventing millions of Americans from becoming financially independent. To see what I mean, we must step back into history and observe how credit was developed, for what purpose, who was affected by it, and how it's affecting us today.

A Brief History on Credit

Credit, the predominant way of conducting business today, wasn't always available. Prior to the 1700s, the system didn't exist. Yet people survived. After the 1700s, however, merchants found it increasingly difficult to stay in business without having to extend credit to the average man.

By extending credit, the system achieved two goals: (1) merchants were able to move their inventory and (2) cash-poor people found a way to purchase merchandise and pay later. And so, the installment-credit system was born.

Installment Credit

In some ways, installment credit may appear to have solved an economic problem, at least for both merchants and cash-poor people. But unfortunately, the practice was reserved for a few individuals: only those in dire straits had access to the system. Most people avoided it because the practice exposed the poorest class in the community. Any association with the use of credit in those days was embarrassing. So much so that business owners such as butchers, cabinetmakers, and grocers kept credit transactions well documented but highly private.

In time, however, more and more people started using credit to buy the things they needed. Like today, they purchased furniture, groceries, and even real estate on credit. In time, the practice became more acceptable, and the shame associated with the use of credit gradually dissipated.

Meanwhile, the careless and poorest in the community started abusing the system. Though much of it was unintentional, personal circumstances caused them to use more credit than they could afford to pay, making it difficult to honor the contract agreement.

Merchants, on the other hand, had little patience and sympathy for those who defaulted on credit arrangements. For instance, prior to the Revolutionary War of 1775 with Great Britain, Americans were being put in jail for debt as little as $0.50.

Mind you, debtors' prison was no fun. The rooms were small and usually crowded. The typical sight was considered horribly dirty and grossly nauseating for both visitors and inmates. Historical accounts told of the fear, torture, torments, and even death of those who were incarcerated in those jails. Given these conditions, one would think that people would be discouraged from using credit. But that wasn't the case. Some people had become helplessly dependent on the system and saw no other way to survive. In the process, they risked the possibility of going to jail. In 1758, Samuel Johnson wrote the following:

> *"It is vain to continue an institution whose experience shows to be ineffectual. We have now imprisoned one generation of debtors after another, but we do not find that their numbers lessen. We have now learned that rashness and imprudence will not be deterred*

from taking credit; let us try whether fraud and avarice may be more easily restrained from giving it."

Considering the nature of credit and the punishment awarded to those who fail to honor their contracts, such an environment would cater to people only of little or no reputation—bums and deadbeats, for example. On the contrary, people who got credit in those days were those who appeared to have great means to repay the debt. For example, Charles Goodyear was put in jail for four days because he was unable to pay his debt to his distributors.

Robert Morris was also imprisoned for bad debt. He was one of the founding fathers of this country, a man whom George Washington depended on for financial assistance. In addition to financing the 1776 American Revolution, Robert Morris provided clothing, food, supplies, and ammunition for the troops. He borrowed money against his assets and negotiated loans with the French to finance the war.

But despite the fact that he was appointed by Congress as the superintendent of finance, he lacked self-discipline and good judgment with his own personal finances. Consequently, in 1798, he was incarcerated for shady land deals. Later, he was released as a result of the National Bankruptcy Law passed in 1802.

With deteriorating health, broken spirit, and evaporated assets, Robert Morris walked out of prison into poverty. Congress later remembered his contribution and pardoned his transgression. His portrait was eventually placed on the 1880 ten-dollar bill as a token of appreciation.

Obviously, these men were not the only two known victims whose lives were destroyed by credit. There were countless others. Yet it seems that even with the most severe punishment, the system was destined to survive. With eye-popping inventions and little or no cash to purchase them, people were encouraged to use credit as a means to get what they wanted.

For example, in 1850, millions of women became obsessed with the sewing machine because of its labor-saving capability. A shirt that used to take fifteen hours to complete could be finished in one hour on the sewing machine. With $1 down and $4 a month, Singer sold millions of $30 sewing machines on installment credit. Situations like these pushed people to demand easier access to credit. Meanwhile, merchants welcomed the opportunity to serve those with the ability to pay their debt.

By 1920, the shame associated with the use of credit was completely gone. At that time, 80 percent of all stereo equipment, 75 percent of laundry equipment (washers and dryers), 65 percent of house-cleaning utilities, and 25 percent of jewelry were bought on installment credit.

As one can imagine, the installment credit explosion wasn't altogether positive. As people continued to rely more and more on the system, many of them eventually got trapped by it. And those who didn't end up in jail ended up losing their valuable possessions.

In time, the abuse of credit give rise to a new voice. Groups such as the Puritans saw credit as a contradiction and started talking about the system. As far as they were concerned, the ability to use credit was a sign of trustworthiness and dependability. Yet the inability to pay the debt was a sign from hell. It depicted a flawed character and a lack of credibility. The following is a perspective from the 1800s:

> *"Credit is one of the beneficial fruits of Christian civilization and, though itself an effect, is in turn the most powerful agent in developing the resources of nations and accelerating their progress. But to contract debts without a reasonable prospect of being able to pay them when they become due is both a sin and a sure source of perplexity and trouble."*

Evidently, the abuse of credit prompted this reaction from the Puritans. By this time, more and Americans were experiencing the destruction of credit. Those who hadn't gotten trapped by the system had seen or heard about others who had. And so, for many, credit was both a bitter and sweet phenomenon. It meant having access to the most basic products and services. Yet, many had difficult paying their debt, creating a financial nightmare.

Long-term Credit

Prior to 1950, *long-term* credit (loans for houses, cars, boats, etc.) was short-lived. Home and vehicle loans lasted no more than twelve months. At that time, bankers approved loans to people with adequate collateral, and local butchers and grocers extended lines of credit to people who were dependable and honest.

This type of restrictive approach to long-term credit wasn't unusual, however, because during the fifties, people were optimistically cautious about the future. While the impact of The Great Depression still lingered in consumers' minds, lenders began to recall the great risk associated with lending. In the thirties, they were forced to repossess farms, businesses, and homes that were almost worthless. And somehow, they feared something similar might happen again.

However, this attitude would soon change. After W.W. II, the country faced an extraordinary challenge. Millions of veterans came back home wanting jobs, education, and housing. Still cautious, bankers were reluctant in advancing loans to people with no collateral and credit history. As a result, Congress intervened and passed the GI Bill, which allowed banks to extend housing and educational credit to millions of military personnel.

With the federal government guaranteeing loans for homes, education, and businesses, millions of people took advantage of the opportunity. Then the credit boom was created by people who wanted to go back to school, build houses, and start businesses. The program was later expanded to include nonmilitary personnel through other government agencies such as the Federal Farm Loan Administration (FFLA), Federal Housing Administration (FHA), and the Small Business Administration (SBA). Banks got onboard as well, and *long-term* loans became a common product.

The collaboration between government and the private sector did a lot of good. The arrangement reignited an economic explosion like no one had seen. Accordingly, people regained their confidence in the credit system, and the demand for goods and services increased. And again, this move was good for business.

With the economic expansion came inflation. Prices of goods and services increased beyond the reach of some consumers. Then people began losing their homes at a rapid pace, prompting lenders to react swiftly.

In the process of trying to curb the problem, banks implemented more stringent loan criteria, one of which was the 25 percent rule. For example, home-loan qualification was limited to only 25 percent of total household income, a policy that almost paralyzed the real-estate, appliance, construction, and automobile industries. This situation lasted for several years until the early sixties.

Then, in the mid-sixties, a new group of young people was introduced to the banking industry. Compared to The Great Depression generation, they were more flexible and aggressive. The younger group quickly realized that more loans had to be made to get the economy moving again. Determined to make a difference, they modified the 25 percent rule by extending the loan period, which created smaller payments on long-term debt. This modification enabled people with smaller incomes to qualify for home loans.

By the 1970s, Americans had a renewed faith in the credit system. Literally, every economic group depended on credit as a way of life. Then, more than before, Americans began using credit to purchase food, clothes, medicines, and more. Additionally, they began borrowing against the appreciated value on their homes and businesses for more financial leverage, a practice that continued to fuel the economy.

At the same time, lenders continued to look for additional solutions to financial security. In the process, they augmented the 25 percent rule to 40 percent and became more lenient with customers. Car loans were extended to sixty months, which provided an opportunity for Americans without assets to qualify for loans.

Revolving Credit

Revolving credit is the most popular system used today. Yet no one knows for sure its time of origin. The best established time is 1951 when Franklin National Bank first released a credit card. Subsequently, other lending institutions followed suit, flooding the market with credit cards.

Since then, revolving credit has been a preferred method of borrowing money. Unlike installment debt where a consumer creates a new account every time he or she qualifies for a loan, with revolving credit, one can borrow money, repay it, and borrow again without having to requalify.

People as young as eighteen years old with less than perfect credit and no collateral were able to take advantage of this opportunity. Therefore, because of its flexibility, revolving credit has become the main choice by which most Americans conduct business.

Present-day Credit

Today, credit hasn't changed much except the system has become more sophisticated. Financial institutions have become quite versed in creating new ways to package money in order to meet the financial needs of Americans.

The interesting thing is, in addition to being accustomed to the system, we've actually grown to love it just like the generations before us. One of the main reasons is that credit provides us the opportunity to achieve our fantasies. Since the majority of us lack the discipline to accumulate cash to buy what we need, credit has become the substitute. Today, we use the system to buy literally everything we *need* and *want*.

But with all of its attractiveness, credit has remained true to its nature, meaning, like a venomous snake, it has held on to its deadly sting. Each year, millions of Americans are becoming financially incapacitated as a result of its bite, mainly because the majority of us have been misinformed about its true identity or have become careless with its use.

The Credit Identity Crisis

Whenever I get the opportunity during a workshop or speaking engagement, I often ask my audience the following question, "When you use credit, whose money are you using?"

The answer I get may surprise you. "My money," some would say. "The bank's money," others would reply. "The credit card company's money," others would respond. And finally, "Our money," yet another group would reply.

For the most part, few people care about the source of borrowed money when applying for credit. The purpose for which the money is being used is usually more exciting than the money itself. On the other hand, it's quite fascinating to see the volume of people who lack the concept of borrowed money. In fact, roughly 80 percent of my young audience believed that borrowed money belongs to the user. What's wrong with this picture?

On the contrary; seldom will I hear someone say that borrowed money belongs to other people—people who have deliberately invested their money in banks, credit unions, brokerage houses, etc. for profits.

Then, the accumulated funds get loaned out to people who feel the need to borrow (see figure 11.1).

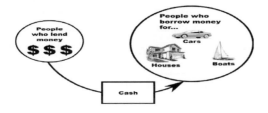

Fig. 11.1

Believing that borrowed money belongs to the user is a gross misconception about credit. Yet this notion is spread through the minds of too many Americans, particularly the younger groups. No wonder most of us use credit as though we've earned the money. We use it for trips, vacations, and a myriad of other things with little concern about the inability to pay it back.

This delusional view about credit needs our attention because it consistently gets people into financial trouble. With all the limitations of cash having been stripped away, credit cards shopping becomes a flexible and gratifying experience. One can only imagine careless and impulsive spenders, for example, leisurely buying items simply for recreational purposes. It's like taking advantage of free money for unnecessary spending. This type of thinking is particularly prevalent in government. Some departments feel that they must spend the extra money on the budget simply because it's available. So they buy unnecessary items for the joy of spending.

The same is true for credit card shopping. The activity is somewhat illusive. Psychologically, the transaction remains a fantasy until the bill comes due at the end of the month. It is only then that some people realize that they've been spending money that must be paid back.

The Obligation

Shopping is fun. A good amount of it, when done within the context of one's budget, is an ecstasy for most of us. However, once the shopping is over, so is the fun. At that point, if most of what is purchased is bought with credit, then we're faced with the aspect of credit we all love to hate: the "debt."

Unfortunately, we have a tendency to forget that debt comes with the deal. Again, this phase of the program is usually surprised or ignored during shopping until the end of the experience. This happens because the thought of being unable to pay the bill interrupts the joy of shopping.

This attitude is a direct result of good advertisement. It is the intent of those who promote the use of credit to hide its potential harm and magnify its good qualities. At first, the system presents itself as a savior. For example, bankers, credit-card companies, and mortgage brokers advertise credit as the solution to all our financial aches and pains. "Credit cards," they say, "are everywhere you go, and they're good for every situation." But as soon as we buy into the deal, the relationship changes. Those of us who use the system suddenly become *indentured servants* to the lender, a relationship that stays undisclosed until one buys into the agreement.

Yet this is the main intent of creditors. We become legally bound to the lender until the debt is repaid. Therefore, from that moment forward until the entire loan balance is paid off, the lender sees the borrower as a *profit center,* an endless source of income for the duration of the loan. The borrower is not only obligated to pay the principal amount of the loan, but also the interest charged on the borrowed money, which becomes income or profit to the lender (see figure 11.2).

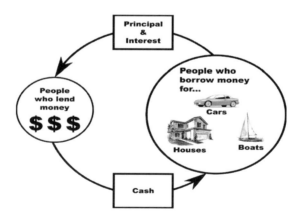

Fig. 11.2

When you look at the picture from this angle, it's easy to see who benefits the most with credit. It is, of course, the lender. The one who collects interest payments from you every month stands to make a lot of money for as long as you owe a balance on the debt. Also, it stands to reason that the higher the balance, the more money the lender makes from you.

So a company that's in the business of lending money needs to simply flood the market with loans. By doing so, it has the opportunity to create an unlimited amount of income.

The goal of every credit card company in this country, for example, is to turn every American worker into a *profit center.* This is accomplished by giving a loan or credit card to each person and wait for payments. And so it is, as you read this portion of this book, each credit card company is positioning itself to recruit as many Americans as possible into its own credit card database. Obviously, the one with the most members makes the most money.

Again, looking back at figure 11.2, which circle would you say that most Americans occupy: the bigger circle or the smaller one? If you say the bigger circle, you're absolutely right, in which case, the equation is simple. Economically, there is a small group of people with lots of money who are ready to lend to the majority of Americans—the bigger circle. In return, the people in the bigger circle pay interest (income) continually to those in the smaller circle. The interesting thing is, unless those who are in the bigger circle change their dependency from credit usage, they'll remain *indentured servants* (in debt and broke) to those in the smaller circle: the wealthy—a stunning revelation but true.

The financial obligation continues long after the joy of shopping vanishes. Meanwhile, it makes no difference to the lender what economic hardship a borrower runs into. The reality is, that person must pay the loan obligation based on contract agreement or else.

Unfortunately, this is when the burden of excessive credit becomes extremely heavy. Suddenly, credit takes on a different form. It turns into debt, which becomes a millstone around the necks of millions of Americans. In fact, this situation reminds me of a bumper sticker in the nineties that read, "I owe, I owe, so off to work I go." Funny, but real.

For all I know, this bumper sticker no longer exists. Yet the message is just as poignant today as ever. The truth is, millions of us are weighted down with excessive debt. The worse of it is that each day, the weight gets heavier, making it difficult to rest comfortably. This is a *financially checkmate* position.

The Credit Threat

Lately, millions of Americans have come to realize that the embellished appearance of credit is to be respected because hidden within its flamboyancy is also the potential for great pain. As such, one should never forget the contradiction when dealing with the system.

It is true that many people have prospered through the use of credit. Yet more have perished by the system. And while it's true that few people go to debtors' prisons these days, many have come close to doing jail time. For instance, each year, over a million people seek bankruptcy protection, trying to preserve some form of personal dignity as they face the wrath of creditors. Yet millions more are struggling to keep their heads above water as they try to find ways to consolidate debts, hoping to avert becoming credit casualties themselves.

It is this type of threat that hangs over the heads of millions of Americans as they try to enjoy life. The fear of possibly losing everything at any given moment is real. We've watched some of our friends and neighbors who once had a great lifestyle and suddenly became homeless. Others who are being hounded by creditors day and night because they can't pay their debts. Yet others who are being denied the opportunity to use credit as a result of damaged reputations.

The need to keep creditors at bay has become our number one focus as we work for the dollar. The thought of not having a job or an income to pay the mortgage, the car payments, and all the other essentials that we've purchased on credit takes the joy out of life. Worse, after years and years of paying debts, we get the feeling that we simply exist to do nothing else but that. In the meantime, someone, somewhere, is profiting from our pain. He or she is making a lot of money from our mortgage payments and other debts.

Frankly, I'm not sure which is worse: debtors' prison or a lifetime of debt obligations.

Recommendations for Credit Users

There is no doubt that the credit system occupies a valuable place in our economic system. Without it, America wouldn't be as affluent as it is today. Everyone makes a contribution into the system: the government borrows money for projects and war; corporations borrow money for expansion and financial balance; entrepreneurs borrow money for new ventures; and individuals borrow money for consumption.

But the cost of borrowing is not cheap. Everyone who borrows money must pay the interest due (the cost of borrowed money). While a few people or companies benefit from borrowed money, some people lose big. Those who do are generally individual consumers who use credit for day-to-day living.

As a consumer, you're responsible to not only understand how the credit system works, but also how to protect your well-being. There is no need to avoid using the system entirely. But each time you do, you should cringe about the fact that you're using someone's money to improve your personal situation. If you have a need to use credit, use only what you need and no more.

Any extra use of credit could be economically fatal. The system will use you instead of you using it. For example, if you keep the economy healthy by spending excessively on credit, economists and investors will love you for it. But you could be doing it to your own peril. Yet the same economy won't care one way or another if you perish in the process. It will simply keep moving on, leaving you behind to mend your broken life.

So be wise. Find a way to remove yourself from the large circle and into the small one (See figures 11.1 and 11.2) in this chapter. Do the lending instead of the borrowing. This option will be more profitable and personally rewarding.

CHAPTER 12

Autoculture Economy

(Cultural Trap No. 7)

The economy, as you know, is a commercial environment that pulls together resources of all types and turn them into commodities. More specifically, it's a system of cooperative efforts involving raw materials such as people's talents, land, equipment, buildings, and capital to generate *goods* and *services* for consumption.

Every culture has its economic system, one that's suitable for its needs. Few, however, replicate the model we have. Ours is a progressive, intuitive system that seems to have a life of its own. In fact, we speak of the economy as though it were a separate entity, an independent detached system composed of a visible image with body, soul, and spirit.

But the economy cannot act on its own. It has no mind or self-intelligence like some would make us believe. So it needs our involvement in order to function properly. As such, one can visualize the economy as a commercial playground where people transact business consistently, a place where the rich, the middle class, and the poor come together to make a living.

In this commercial arena, everyone is required to make an initial deposit, usually one that involves dollars and cents or a by-product that ultimately converts into money. Then, all day long, the economic wheel turns. And as it does, it takes and it gives. At the end of the day, when the dust is settled, the rich usually get richer, and the poor get poorer.

The Economy *Giveth* and the Economy *Taketh* Away

If you haven't attained your financial goals to this point, it could be that you have been manipulated by the economy all those years. The system is cunning, smart, and heartless. It has a tendency to create an environment that puts you at ease and make you feel that it's working in your favor. But it could be taking advantage of you in broad daylight without you realizing it. The interesting thing is, it has the ability to out-maneuver the financially unprepared and naive individuals among us, and it happens everyday.

The Income Benefactor

The economy is a master of job creation. At any given time and place in this culture, one can always find a way to make money. From ditch digging, avocado picking, computer engineering, aeronautics, and anything in between, there's always something a person can do to earn a dollar. What's even more encouraging is that as long as we live in this country, the economy will continue to provide jobs.

The job-generating system itself isn't hard to understand. Initially, everything starts with people's *needs* and *wants*. The desire to have more or better goods and services has been the main thrust behind the economic wheel.

Entrepreneurs are usually the ones who take the leadership role in bringing everything together. They are, by nature, people who love to take risks and get rewarded for their bravery. As a result, their eyes are always open looking for ways to improve people's lives through business. If they can't find a need, they create one. They simply watch people, observe their behavior, and respond accordingly.

Assume, for instance, that an entrepreneur has a business idea that needs pursuing. In most cases, the individual may not be able to perform all the necessary functions of the business. Depending on the type of operation, functions may include, but are not limited to, research and development, marketing and distribution, finance and accounting, human resources, etc. People with special skills in these areas must be hired to perform the duties. Suddenly jobs are created.

Imagine for a moment that this type of activity is taking place all around the country at the same time. Jobs of various types from multiple companies are being made available to the public. When people get hired to perform a service, they usually get paid for their contributions.

The form of payment varies, depending on the role of the individual in the company. For example, some people get paid through salaries or wages, some are paid by commission, and others are paid through profits.

Job creations and payment for services alone do not complete the economic cycle. The system needs more key components in the equation: the wages, salaries, profits, and all the other forms of payments we earn through the economy. These eventually go right back into the cycle through expenditures. That's right. The same producers of goods and services become consumers of the various products and services they provide. It is this phenomenon that completes and maintains an economic system, an endless system of commerce.

Keep in mind that if the money doesn't go back into the economy, the system will freeze or halt, making it difficult for people to find jobs and make money.

The Income Sapper

The income we get from the economy is everything. It pays for shelter, transportation, food, clothes, and countless other things in our lives. These needs go on forever. It makes sense, therefore, that as long as these needs exist, money should always be available to pay for them.

Therefore, our income should be divided into two major portions: some for the present and the rest for the future. For most of us, however, it doesn't work that way. Each day, we're encouraged by the economy to spend every dollar we make now (the present) while we neglect the future. The worse part is we generally act on the suggestions, a situation that leaves us in a state of always needing money to spend and never having enough to save. This type of arrangement is good for the economy but bad for us, because while the economy remains bullish as a result of our excessive spending, most of us stay broke.

The way it happens is very simple. First, the economy appears to be considerate by providing jobs. Then it imposes income limitations on all workers through job classification. For example, all engineers make about the same amount of money. All teachers get paid roughly the same salary. The same is true for automobile mechanics, computer programmers, laborers, military personnel in the same rank, truck drivers, and so on. The slight difference in pay from one individual to another in the same field of work has to do with the degree of experience. Otherwise, all employees are marked with a specific salary or wage. In other words, the economy says to all of us, "Sure, I'll give you a job. But as long as you perform this specific function, you'll earn this much money and no more."

So clearly, the economy retains control over how much we make. Since the economy has a parasitic nature, it needs the same money it gives us in order to continue thriving. And if we allow it to do so, it will take every dime back from us without remorse.

Remarkably, it remains unbiased with its tricks. Everyone is treated the same way regardless of income. One who makes $30,000 a year is treated the same way as one who generates $300,000 a year. It devours every dime at the same rate—quickly.

One of my client's situations comes to mind: A couple with a combined income of $90,000 a year struggled from paycheck to paycheck. After several years of trying to hold things together, they got concerned about their current situation as well as their financial future. Somewhat perplexed about their predicament, they finally came to me for some answers. Every dollar they made went into expenses, and they still ran a deficit each month. In other words, the economy was sucking back from them all their income and then some.

This problem is far from being unusual. This is exactly what's happening to millions of Americans all over the United States. The strange thing is, they don't know how they got there, and worse, they have no idea how to get out of the situation.

Hopefully, the following section will shed some light on this type of financial entrapment.

The Home Ownership Illusion

For most of us, it starts with the house or real-estate issue. For years, we're being told that home ownership is one of the wisest financial investments one can make for the future. Bankers, accountants, and real estate brokers have raved about the benefits that come with home ownership. Along with the stability and pride of owning a home, one gets the opportunity to stop throwing away money in rent. But more importantly, one can write off the mortgage interest while building some equity on the house, thus, creating wealth in the process.

For most Americans, the opportunity to write off taxes and build equity at the same time makes good economic sense, and home ownership provides the perfect solution. Consequently, the purchase of a home has become our number one priority—the ultimate goal. Therefore, when the housing opportunity comes, we usually jump on it as though it is the final conquest in life.

But is there any negative issue associated with home buying? It certainly doesn't seem that way given the pitch and passion through which the idea is conveyed to the masses. Yet few homeowners are better off financially than non-homeowners. Worse, for some, the longer they own a house, the poorer they become.

One of the main reasons, of course, is the heavy financial burden that comes with home ownership. The heaviest is the responsibility of the home mortgage. For most homeowners, this will be the biggest debt obligation they'll ever make, one that will keep them trapped in financial bondage for years. Still few people see it that way because most of us are trained to look at the home ownership issue only from a positive angle: the appreciated value and the tax write-off.

On the other hand, this concept will never be presented to the public any other way. Too many people stand to benefit from the sale of a house—most of whom are major players in our culture such as bankers, real-estate attorneys, real-estate brokerage houses, escrow companies, cities, counties and the states, to name a few. In short, the business of real estate is the most lucrative aspect of the economy. And because of this, the message will continue to be positive.

But what about the homeowners? Are they benefiting from the deal? Not much. Consider the following situation. Assume that you're in the market to buy a house. You and your spouse have a combined gross income of $100,000 a year and have decided to buy a house. You choose the location in which you want to live and find a real-estate agent to assist you with the purchase.

Prior to taking you on a house hunt, however, the agent will prequalify you to determine your range of purchase. This is something commonly done in the industry. Based on your combined income, you may qualify for a house between $250,000 (low-end) to $450,000 (high-end).

Additionally, your financial viability must be taken into account. This is done by examining three critical areas of your life:

1. Your income stability—how long you and your spouse have been working in your current field,
2. Your creditworthiness—how well you have you paid your debts in the past, and
3. Your debt-to-income ratio—how much debt you currently have compared to your income

When these conditions are met satisfactorily, you'll be permitted to proceed with the purchase.

By this time, assuming that you haven't picked out a house, the agent will take you through various neighborhoods to look for one. In your case, the agent may start at the bottom price range and work upward. As you go through the search, you'll find homes that you like in the $250,000 to $350,000 range. But ultimately, you will fall in love with a $450,000 house. So you'll buy it, thinking that you can afford it.

In order to buy the $450,000 house, however, you may be required to make some adjustments, one of which might be a $40,000 down payment. Since it's unlikely to have this much cash on hand, you'll most likely go to your 401(k) retirement plan to get it. Additionally, you may be required to pay off some credit card debts to lower your debt-to-income ratio.

If you're able to fulfill both of these requirements, in approximately ninety days after opening escrow, you'll walk into your brand-new $450,000 house. Prior to closing escrow, however, something caught your attention. You noticed that your mortgage payments—including *principal, interest, taxes,* and *insurance* (PITI)—will be $3,702.94 each month. You may have flinched when you saw the figure, but you ignored it. This payment, of course, will be your biggest monthly debt obligation—ever. Nevertheless, you went through with the deal, thinking that somehow you'll manage to pay the mortgage.

Meanwhile, you're completely oblivious of the fact that you've gone over your head in debt. Ideally, a $250,000 house would have been a more prudent investment in your situation. But instead, you made an unreasonable financial judgment by purchasing a house worth $450,000.

Don't feel bad. Most of us would do exactly what you did. In fact, that's the problem. Most Americans don't understand the real estate business. Yet we impulsively rush to a decision when buying houses. This type of reaction, of course, is directly attributed to the culture. Here is why:

1. We've all been programmed to think that bigger is better, particularly in this situation. There is more value in a bigger house than a smaller one. The backyard is larger, the extra room is more convenient, and the vaulted ceiling is more attractive,

2. We get emotionally trapped when buying a house and don't want to let go, even when the financial arrangement implies trouble ahead. For instance, we tend to disregard the inflated mortgage payment thinking that our financial condition will improve to sustain it,

2. We want others to see our accomplishments. Bragging rights are important among friends and neighbors, and we want to be the top dog.

3. The real estate agent fans the flames of possibilities. After all, the agent's personal interest is at stake here. Since a 6 percent commission is larger on $450,000 than $250,000, you'll be encouraged to buy the bigger house.

Having purchased the $450,000 house, you've put yourself in a compromising financial position. You just haven't noticed it because you're still excited about your new home. You've gotten the house you've always wanted and, for the next few months, you'll be busy putting it together. Like most of us, you'll be buying new carpet, sprinkler systems, lighting fixtures, curtains and rods, plants and fences, and many other amenities.

Unfortunately, most of these purchases will be paid for on credit cards. A recent survey pointed out that Americans spend an average of $10,000 on their homes in first year. Most of that money got spent with credit cards. So you'll end up doing the same thing. You now have a house, but you're most likely cash poor. The only difference is, you haven't started to feel it—yet.

The Car Factor

Success, as you know, feeds on itself. Even the appearance of success is sometimes enough to inspire people to do more. We simply get motivated by the hype and keep acting in a way consistent with our feelings. That's one of the reasons we keep spending money when the economy is doing well even when it's not financially prudent to do so.

Shortly after moving into the new house, you got the urge to buy a new vehicle. Your justification is simple: you're making progress, and your circumstances necessitate the change. Frankly, you feel uncomfortable parking the jalopy in your new driveway. It gives your neighbors the wrong impression. Furthermore, it's hard to convince yourself, or anyone else for that matter, that you're making progress while driving a five or six year-old car.

So you drove down to your favorite car dealership to buy a new vehicle. Roughly six hours later, you're driving home with a $25,000 car. By this time, you're in heaven. You have a new house, a new car, and a great attitude.

Keep in mind, however, that you haven't taken a serious look at your budget. In the last few months, you've been busy with homeowner's issues and had little time to notice that your financial situation was getting worse.

Roughly eight months after all these evolutions, you're struggling to make ends meet. Even after cutting back on food, utilities, recreation, and all the extras, you can barely come up with enough money to handle everything. Seemingly, your combined paychecks are just enough to pay the mortgage. Suddenly, you're feeling choked financially and don't know why.

Outmaneuvered by the Economy

Living from paycheck to paycheck wasn't your idea of living a successful life. You've invested too much time and money for education and training hoping to prevent that from happening. Yet lately, your condition seems to have gotten worse since you bought the house and the new car. So what happened?

Could it be that you never had control over your financial affairs in the first place? My impression is that the economy has always controlled your situation, and you haven't realized it until now. For instance, initially, the economy gave you $100,000 in combined annual income. Yet it made you spend more than $120,000 a year.

"How is this possible?" you ask. It's easy. Most of us are aware of the fact that we spend more money than we make. How much more remains a mystery for a lot of people. But Americans spend $1.20 to every $1.00 they make. The extra comes from credit cards and other forms of credit, as you can imagine. In other words, the economy took back 100 percent of the income it gave you. Then, it forced you to spend more by allowing you to borrow additional funds.

But specifically, how did the economy manipulate you during your biggest financial conquest? The reality is that you simply became oblivious of the facts. Consider some of the following mistakes you made:

- Your house purchasing eligibility was evaluated based on your gross income ($100,000).
- Your mortgage, car payment, and all other financial issues relating to your lifestyle were paid using net income. In your case, that would be roughly $85,000.
- Your ideal house purchase price should have been close to $250,000. Instead, you stretched your budget and bought a house valued at $450,000, your biggest mistake.
- You compounded the problem by purchasing a new vehicle without thoroughly considering your budget.
- Furthermore, you purchased additional amenities for the house on credit cards, increasing your debt load even more.

To all intents and purposes, it's possible to get away with this type of situation once in a lifetime. But unfortunately, for many Americans, this problem is repeated every seven to ten years, making it difficult to get ahead financially.

The bottom line is, the majority of us make extremely high financial commitments on houses and cars and spend the rest of our lives working to pay for them.

You're Not Alone

It's easy to think that the only people who get trapped by the economy are those at the lower income level. But that's not true. The economy manipulates individuals at all income levels.

For instance, don't be surprised that your banker may not have available cash in his checking account for emergencies; the individual who is helping you consolidate your debt has just applied for a loan for the same reason; the loan officer who's preparing the loan documents for your house can't qualify for a mortgage loan because of low credit scores; the financial planner who sits behind a desk in a high-rise building, ready to tell you where to invest your money, wishes she had some money to invest as well.

As I write, I'm reminded of a couple of situations that fit this condition. A loan officer friend recently admitted her financial dilemma to me. "Frankly," she said, "I make well above two hundred thousand dollars a year but have no idea where the money goes." This is a common complaint at all financial levels. My friend went on to say that if she needed a loan, she would avoid going to her own bank to get it. "Personally," said my friend, "I'm embarrassed about my financial situation, and I couldn't let people who know me well examine it. I would lose my credibility with them."

By the way, this individual is not financially dense. Each year, she approves millions of dollars in home loans for others and stays informed about the financial market. Yet she stays broke and struggles financially.

Another banker who spoke with me on the phone had a similar experience. Again, another paradox. "Here I am, making loans for people," he said, "and I can't even qualify for one myself." Certainly, these two situations are not out of the ordinary. Based on what we've covered so far, it's easy to see how people can get trapped by the economy regardless of how much money they make each year.

Moreover, people who claim to be well-versed in finance ironically get manipulated by the same economy. One of my clients is a budget analyst who managed millions of dollars on a daily basis. Each day, she made sure that all her accounts are up-to-date and balanced. Yet her personal financial situation was falling apart. She was absolutely mortified to admit that to me. But then again, she needed help.

Minority Rules

There are exceptions to every rule, however, and this economic juxtaposing is no different. Some people get to maintain control over their economic situation. They make the economy work for them instead of having it the other way around. These individuals are a small group of people consisting of roughly 10 percent of the American population.

Call them the rich or well-to-do. The truth is, they've learned how the economy works, and they use it to their advantage.

Recommendations

You need to do the same. Among other things, you need to avoid over-extending when purchasing houses and cars, the two most decapitating financial blunders we make on a consistent basis.

The bottom line is that you need to learn how to take more from the economy than what you allow it to have.

PART III

Solutions to the Problem

"Money, it turned out, was exactly like sex, you thought of nothing else if you didn't have it and thought of other things if you did."

JAMES BALDWIN (1924-1987).
*Nobody Knows My Name: More Notes of a
Native Son, 13, 1961.*

HOW TO MASTER THE
MONEY GAME TO WIN

To this point, we've established the fact that you, like the rest of us, want to be financially independent. So much so that you've done all the necessary preparation to accomplish this goal. You've gone to college for a degree; you've been hired by some of the most prestigious companies in this country; you've earned the promotions and the job titles you wanted; and you've made a lot of money in the process. Based on your possessions, it appears that you've attained the American dream. Yet for those who can see through the façade, you are broke or cash poor.

My guess is that you've become more aware of your financial predicament. You now know that the economic culture has distracted you from your intended goal. Beginning with Chapter 5, you saw some of the things we do as a culture while progressing through time. Instead of charting our own individual courses in life, most of us simply follow a common path taken by the majority of people.

On this path, we participate in specific cultural habits, rituals, or customs. Many of these functions appear to be normal behavior designed to improve our lives. Nevertheless, they impede our financial progress unknowingly. In Chapters 6-12, we identified seven distinct cultural hindrances to financial prosperity. Some of which are summarized below:

1. the issue of children growing up in this country and reaching adulthood without sound financial knowledge;
2. our belief and value system that sometimes works quietly against our mission in life, hindering us from developing our true potential;
3. an educational system that places the wrong set of values on a college degree that carries little or no substance, and it seems like everyone else profits from a college investment except the person who made the sacrifice;

4. employers who hire people for work but place a salary cap on their income—an ongoing source of frustration for millions of people because while their *needs* and *wants* increase, their salaries stay flat;

5. government taxes that intrusively devour between 30 to 60 percent of people's income, and the remaining portion is barely enough to take care of financial responsibilities in the home;

6. a credit system that makes itself available to everyone who is struggling with a cash problem. At first, the system appears to be friendly, making itself the answer to all financial woes, yet quickly turns its users into indentured servants;

7. an economic system that provides jobs or income yet takes everything back from those who allow it. So while it provides 100 percent income for those with jobs, it takes back 120 percent from them through spending.

Year after year, we work hard trying to make more progress. Yet as time passes, we find ourselves with less financial stability. Meanwhile, the economy prospers from our inputs.

If we've created an economic culture for our benefit, why do most of us feel used by it? Think about it: as we spend our hard earn money, the economy gets "bullish" (hot and healthy). The more we spend, the more upbeat it gets. When this happens, manufacturing and distribution skyrocket, jobs are created, economists get excited, and investors make money. Unfortunately, a great deal of these activities are generated by consumers who used credit to purchase items and, many times, reaching far beyond their spending limits in the process.

The indiscriminant economy doesn't necessarily care how items are purchased—cash or credit. That concern is left strictly to the consumer's discretion. But few American shoppers think about their budgets or spending limits while shopping. So, the economy takes and keeps taking from us until all, or most, of our resources (cash or credit) are depleted.

When that happens, we become financially incapacitated. Sometimes this occurs as a result of excessive credit, job loss, illness, or other misfortunes. At that time, we can no longer contribute to the economic culture and, consequently, we get discarded as damaged goods. Then we get placed in dilapidated warehouses in our society. There, as a result of damaged FICO scores, bankruptcies, and repossessions, we're left at the mercy of predatory lenders who take advantage of our injured conditions.

As a consumer, you need to take this situation to heart because your economic success depends on it. Realistically, you need to reevaluate your relationship with the economic culture. Here are some things to consider: are you allowing the economy to take more from you than you can afford? Is it leaving you financially depleted each month and does it expect you to keep working to support it? Or is it working for you, creating an unbelievable amount of success?

If you hesitated in answering these questions, my presumption is that you need some financial guidance. But more specifically, you need to re-examine the importance of money in your life. For example, if your definition of money is simply something you make to spend quickly, you need to change your thinking because this myopic view will keep you broke forever.

You've heard the saying, "Money answers all things." This is certainly true. While it may not raise a family member from the grave, it will do just about everything else.

Knowing this, the job of the economic culture is to garnish all the available cash from your pocket and bank accounts. That's the job of the marketing industry. Each day, it tries to lure you into spending every dime on negligible goods and services—things that have little intrinsic value to your long-term mission in life. Your job, on the other hand, should be to preserve your valuable cash. That means exercising financial prudence in every situation while focusing on your personal interest.

This book, obviously, doesn't claim to have all the answers to financial issues. But it does present direct and non-direct information about money, much of which are essential to building wealth. Many of these concepts, of course, are basic lessons of life that one should have known from youth. Unfortunately, this type information is either ignored or trivialized during that period of life, but without it, achieving financial independence is almost impossible—unless one inherits money.

In the next section, we'll address these issues, hoping that they'll make a positive difference in your life in the future. The ultimate goal is to help you achieve financial independence by the time you retire.

CHAPTER 13

The Terms of Life

No one accomplishes anything in life without first understanding the working conditions. That is, since accomplishments are measured between the points of "start" and "finish," these boundaries (terms) must be set and understood prior to starting the project. Otherwise, one will experience chaos during the process, or at best, an unfinished product or mission.

Every project or situation requires its own set of guidelines, some of which are more simple than others. For instance, a simple rule may suggest that if you want to prevent tooth decay in the future, you must brush your teeth regularly and see the dentist at least once a year. A more difficult situation might stipulate that if you want to cut across the Grand Canyon, you need to know how to apply engineering concepts to build a bridge. Yet another similar situation might propose that before flying to the moon, you need to conceptualize and respect the theory of gravity.

Achieving financial success beyond the ordinary is no different. This process requires a comprehensive view of life's basic lessons, many of which have little to do with money. In fact, some of them are rudiments of life that should be taught to children as toddlers. Moreover, these principles should be reinforced all through life until they become automatic behavior.

But sadly, the majority of American youths have missed many of these principles while growing up. Today's children are growing into adulthood, not knowing the terms and conditions through which people become financially wealthy. Instead, they're being taught concepts that discourage financial independence.

The following ideas may be foreign to you, but they're essential to mastering the game of money.

The Two Phases of Life

To the best of our knowledge, we believe that nature has built time duration in every living thing in the universe. Life, as we know it, goes through a cycle of birth, development, maturity, declination, and, finally, death. This evolution affects not only humans, but also every other living species.

In Chapter 5, we carefully cataloged the developmental stages of human life relative to *time, age,* and *production*—the process of going through life and doing what we do within our allotted time.

As a youth, it's natural to perceive life as an endless existence, in which case, we have unlimited time to do what needs doing. However, it doesn't take long to realize how wrong we are. In fact, as early as our mid-thirties, we realize how quickly the years come and go, leaving us with little time to waste. The older we become, the more distressing the message. Therefore, in relationship to life, time must be treated with utmost respect by using it wisely. For some, the twenty-four-hour day is never enough to get everything done. And although they carefully divide the weeks, months, and years into manageable portions, they still struggle with the reality of running out of time.

On the other hand, some people appear to have too much time on their hands. So they waste it. They "kill time" by accomplishing nothing while admitting to being bored. So while the twenty-four-hour day seems inadequate for some, it's actually too much for others.

There is an easier way to approach the time predicament. And that is, while it may be necessary to divide time into desired fragments, it's also necessary to visualize it in two major segments: (1) a *productive phase* and (2) an *unproductive phase*. Within these two phases of life lies the human limits.

The *productive phase* is viewed in this culture as the working years, a period stretched from age eighteen through sixty-five. During this phase of life, the body remains strong, vibrant, and full of energy. This condition suggests a time of creativity and progress; a time of vision, hope, and possibilities; a time to build and construct; and, most generally, a time to do and keep doing.

Moreover, it is during this phase of life that the body demonstrates the greatest amount of resilience. It has great tolerance for pain, stress, and hard work, and when it's injured, it has the capacity to heal itself quickly.

The *unproductive phase,* on the other hand, is seen as the period from age sixty-five and beyond. This stage of life in this culture represents retirement, a time during which productivity is reduced to a minimum because the body has gotten tired. Time has taken its toll on both mind and body, suggesting pause or rest. *Mentally,* most people are not as sharp as they used to be, and the ability to retain information diminishes. *Physically,* the body begins to lose its stamina. Eyes get blurry, bones get brittle, joints begin to ache, and walking is deliberate and measured. Activities that were once done quickly and easily suddenly become more difficult and, in some cases, impossible. While some people may experience a longer period of strength and functionality during this phase, most people are ready to throw in the towel. They lose the zest for life and decide to simply coast the rest of the way.

Viewing life in these two phases unravels the time mystery. Suddenly, our responsibilities become clearer. For instance, nature has it that during the *productive phase* of life, one should not waste time being aimless, wondering what to do next, but rather take on the responsibility to provide for the *unproductive phase* of life when the body needs rest and relaxation.

Consider the following analogy. The wise King Solomon said:

> *"To everything there is a season and a time for every purpose under heaven: a time to be born, and a time to die; a time to plant, and a time to pluck what is planted; a time to break down, and a time to build up; a time to weep, and a time to laugh; a time to mourn, and a time to dance; a time to cast away stones, and a time to gather stones; a time to embrace, and a time to refrain from embracing; a time to gain, and a time to lose; a time to keep, and a time to throw away; a time to tear, and a time to sew; a time to keep silent, and a time to speak; a time to love, and a time to hate; a time for war, and a time for peace."*

Wow! It doesn't get simpler than this. But then again, few people see life this way.

For all we know, it may not be necessary to fragmentize life to this minute detail. Yet looking within the context of the two phases of life, one begins to realize that there is a good reason to plan wisely and to take action. The ants in your backyard provide a good case in point. Again, King Solomon speaks:

> *"Go to the ant, you sluggard. Consider her ways and be wise, which having no captain, overseer or ruler-provides herself supplies in the summer and gathers her food in the harvest."*

Keep in mind that ants don't get the chance to go to high school or college. So they have no diplomas or degrees. Yet they carefully plan their activities in a sensible fashion. They gather food during the summer and harvest (their productive years), and enjoy it during the winter months when it's cold and rainy. Interestingly enough, ants get no marching orders from parents, supervisors, or bosses. Yet they instinctively do the right thing.

The next time you happen to be in your backyard, observe the ants as they work. They keep everything in order. They create no clutter, no traffic jams, and no confusion. During the summer months, you see heaps and heaps of them everywhere. Yet during the winter season, you see only a handful: the ones that failed to plan.

There is no comparison between humans' and ants' intelligence. Supposedly, human beings are much smarter than ants. Or are we? Because when it comes to providing for the present and planning for the future, it seems like the ants get the message loud and clear. Yet somehow, we still struggle with the problem. In fact, some of us never seem to get the message.

One of the biggest mistakes we make is miscalculating the productive phase of life. We seem to think there is lots of time remaining to get things done, so we procrastinate with our responsibilities while we busy ourselves with trivia. Then at midnight, most often between forty-five and fifty-five years old, we suddenly realize that we're aging fast. And then, we panic.

The surprise isn't so much about the fact that we're aging but more in response to the fact that we have accomplished little or nothing for the past years. And though we remain hopeful that it will happen soon, many lot of us resign to the fact that it's probably too late.

Your Purpose for Living

If you believe that you've been uniquely created or evolved, you should also accept the fact that you were born for a purpose. As such, you have a mission (dream or purpose) to accomplish which is distinctively yours. Therefore, your responsibility in life is to find it and fulfill it because, ultimately, it is that fulfillment that will bring you the most happiness in life.

You should be deliberately searching for that dream. No time should be wasted being bored and aimless but, instead, you should stay focused and determined to find it.

Here is why: Perhaps you hope to live to be ninety years old. In that case, your days are numbered. From birth until death, you have 32,850 days before your life ends. You may think that this is a lot of time, but if you start your mission at twenty years old, you have seventy years left (25,550 days). Furthermore, when you subtract procrastinating time (five years or more), you have sixty-five years remaining. When you take away roughly twenty-five years for rest and comfort (the *unproductive* time of your life), you have approximately forty years remaining to find your purpose and fulfill it. That's roughly 14,600 days.

When you look at your life this way, everything takes on a different meaning. If for no other reason, it gives your life a little bit more value. Imagine, for instance, that we're simply dropped here to drift aimlessly. Your parents would not have invested time and money to raise you. Moreover, you would have little or no motivation to attend college, join the military, stay healthy, go to work, make money, and feed yourself or a family. In short, your life would be boring and extremely useless.

But you know better than that. The fact is, your life contains supreme value. And of course, no one understands this better than your parents. Today, it could be that you're taking your life for granted. However, caring for you initially didn't necessarily come easy. Unless you were born into a rich family, it cost your parents a lot of money to provide you with adequate housing, food, transportation, clothing, health care, child care, and other necessities.

None of these things came cheap, mind you. For instance, according to the U.S. Department of Agriculture (USDA), the 1990-92 financial figures to raise a child from birth to seventeen years old were amazingly high. If you were raised by dual parents who made $39,100 a year before taxes, they spent roughly $124,800 on you; $170,460 if they earned $39,100 to $65,000 a year; and $249,180 if they made more than $65,000 a year before taxes.

You may find these expenses to be somewhat unreal. However, as hard as it is to imagine that so much money was spent on you, that aspect was only part of the cost of raising you. What you didn't see, and, hopefully have come to realize, is the day-to-day sacrifice your parents made on your behalf. For instance, for them, you were first in everything. Consequently, their lives revolved around your needs. Therefore, the time and energy they invested in making sure that you were safe, comfortable, and happy were equally important as scraping a dollar wherever they could find it to buy you shoes. Most of all, they did everything for you with pleasure because they loved you.

The initial investment in your life was no mistake. It was a well-planned and deliberate attempt to prove that your life was *no accident*. As far as your parents were concerned, you were a special bundle of joy uniquely created for greatness. To prove it, they spent roughly eighteen years of their lives making personal sacrifices to convey the message to you.

Admittedly, the investment they made in your life was only the beginning. The idea was to provide enough to raise you to adulthood and then relinquish the responsibilities of your life into your care. At that point, they hoped that you would understand the value of your life, appreciate it, and continue to manage it well. This means, that you would continue to invest in your education, embrace an attitude of progress, maintain a healthy dose of self-esteem, build a boatload of self-confidence, and become widely productive and successful.

How have you measured up to expectations so far? Are you doing as well as your parents expected of you? Are you living up to your personal expectations? Or have you simply folded under the pressures of life and, consequently, are performing less than your potential?

If you're not totally pleased with your progress, it could be that you haven't found your purpose. If so, you have no more time to waste. Continue your search until you find it.

How do you know when you find your purpose? Well, when you find it, life will be exciting again. The "thing" will grab and drive you into action. You'll have a burn in your gut that won't subside until you bring your dream into fruition. You'll be passionate, single-minded, and determined. And although you'll be physically exhausted at times, your mind and body will feed on your excitement and you'll keep going. In that environment, you'll find absolute fulfillment, an experience few people will understand. Yet, it won't matter.

On the other hand, if you don't find your mission or purpose, the alternative is unthinkable. You've heard the saying, "A mind is a terrible thing to waste." I'll say it this way, "A life is a terrible thing to waste."

Until you find your mission, like many people, you'll keep going around in circles every five to ten years. In the process you'll accomplish little or nothing and find yourself going nowhere. Consequently, each year, you'll fall further and further behind, wondering why life is so unfair.

Don't let your life get expended before you find your mission. Stop wasting your valuable time and start taking life seriously. That doesn't mean that you should abandon your responsibilities. But while searching for your purpose in life, you should minimize clutter, imposition on your time, and meaningless tasks that get you nowhere. Instead, work on getting yourself organized and staying focused. By doing so, you'll minimize your regrets as you age.

No One Owes You Anything

"No one owes you anything," is a phrase that you may have heard. Yet, at the time, it meant nothing to you. Meanwhile, you might be quietly hoping that someone, somewhere, owes you something, and you're waiting to collect. If that's the case, may I suggest that you change your outlook on life? This attitude will keep you broke forever. The truth is, until you realize that no one owes you anything, you'll have a hard time accomplishing anything of great value. That includes attaining financial independence.

Frankly, the concept of self-reliance hasn't been a popular theme these days. Lately, fewer people have been exercising their natural abilities to struggle to survive. In fact, it has become more acceptable these days for individuals to associate with groups who are expecting the government, corporations, parents, schools, churches, and insurance companies to make their lives more comfortable and secure. But those who understand the value of self-reliance see people who are wasting their abilities and, ultimately, their lives for a piece of bread.

People who wait for others to do for them are considered victims. This attitude works well for the political system that stands to benefit. Liberal politicians, for instance, love to exploit this theory. Since it provides political clout, they encourage it by making promises they don't intend to keep while promoting class envy at the same time. Yet they care less about the well-being of these poor souls. The sad part is, unless these people change their outlook on life, they'll continually be exploited for political gain.

These politicians are splitting the country apart with little concern for long-term consequences. So far, they've managed to divide our society into two major groups: the haves and the have-nots. By creating these two groups, the idea is to arouse dissension, envy, and hatred between them. Accordingly, those who feel downtrodden and disadvantaged need to simply vote for the politician who promises to take from the rich and give to the poor, supposedly, to even the playing field.

The solution seems simple enough. But why haven't the politicians come through with their promises? And if they have, why haven't people's lives improved? Why are they still poor and feeling victimized even after years of promises? Somehow, things don't add up, particularly for those in question. Yet the same people get voted back into office to continue their political exploitation.

Can we blame the politicians entirely, though? Of course not. In fact, this is a classic case of codependency. Both the politicians and their victims need each other, and all it takes is a vapid promise to bring them together. It's as though the promise itself is what matters most. Meanwhile, the politicians hope that their hollowness never gets discovered as they continue to prey on the ignorance of their victims.

Interestingly enough, the dependency class is not isolated to one segment of our population. This attitude affects people of all ages, gender, and race. It's a disease of the mind, which is highly contagious through social contact, spreading itself from one person to another and from one generation to the next.

Consequently, it's not hard to spot those with the disease. They usually exhibit familiar symptoms such as the tendency to blame others for unfulfilled expectations. Additionally, they're less likely to be grateful when things are given to them. It's as though they expect it and, therefore, deserve it.

I'm reminded of an experience in regards to a specific situation. Recently, my wife and I attended a baby shower and, like many of the invitees, we took an appropriate gift for the occasion. Later that evening, after the introductions and eating, the teenaged couple positioned themselves to open the gifts. One after another, the gifts were unwrapped. In the end, I estimated a value of roughly $1,000 in gifts.

Not once during the event did either of the parents thank those who brought gifts. Did they not appreciate the gifts? I wondered. Or were they disappointed about what they received? Feeling somewhat embarrassed about the situation, the grandmother stepped up to the front and offered her thanks and appreciation to those who attended the event and brought gifts.

Make no mistake. People who expect others to do for them will remain at the bottom of society. They'll make themselves feel content with the "bare minimum," thinking that it's right to live this way. They'll do "just enough" in grade school, in college, at home, in the military, and on the job.

What an unfortunate existence for a human being, one void of personal dignity, respect, and courage. Somehow, these individuals have been taught to believe that "true human excellence" is unattainable. Therefore, they might as well beg or do nothing at all.

Parents who convey this outlook on life to their children are, in fact, doing them a disservice. They're not only destroying their children's potential but also placing a burden on society as well.

Instead, parents should promote positive attributes to their children. Human characteristics such as faith, hope, belief, self-reliance, commitment, and persistence develop children into great human beings. They become dreamers, thinkers, planners, leaders, and positive role models in the community.

Furthermore, children should be taught that no one *deserves* anything unless it's earned. No one deserves an A in school unless he or she works hard to get it; no one deserves a degree unless all requirements are met, e.g. no one deserves a job unless he or she meets all the qualifications; and no one deserves a career with benefits. Nothing is free. A person desiring to have something from government, companies, or any other institution should be prepared to earn it unless it's a gift.

Today, if you desire to attain financial wealth, you need to put a wedge within the fruitless philosophy of dependency. If you don't, you'll remain in the ranks of the poor. You'll end up with nothing better than the crumbs of life and evoking no empathy from anyone.

Furthermore, you'll live a life of continual envy, criticizing those who have more than you. At the same time, you will always hope that your condition will change for the better. But instead, it will remain the same or get worse with time.

The Wealth around You

The aspiration to acquire wealth is not a foreign concept. The idea is rooted in our consciousness just as strongly as the desire to be comfortable secure, and happy. So the desire for wealth has always dominated our psychological presence.

It started the day you were born. Except in the early stages of your life, your parents made sure that your *needs* were met. They provided food, comfort, and safety.

As you grew older, many of your basic *needs* stayed the same except that your appetite for things grew. In time, you no longer desired toys and candy. Instead, you wanted houses, cars, and so on.

Depending on your age, you may have noticed that none of the things you want in life come easy. The main reason is that all of them are owned by other people. All the wealth that you hope for has been acquired by someone else. All the land around you is owned by either a private citizen or the government. The same is true in regards to multicomplex apartment buildings, single family homes, mansions on the hilltops, and so on.

Thinking of wealth in this fashion is sobering. You feel intimidated when you consider that other people control the things you want. Yet there is no other way to see it.

So as you plan to build your empire, you must give a great deal of consideration to your approach. More specifically, your technique should include respect, humility, patience, understanding, and knowledge. The main reason is because you'll be dealing with people who are generally reluctant to relinquish their wealth. Consequently, in addition to having money, you'll need to be smart.

Disregarding this concept and demanding your way to the top will be disappointing. People will avoid you and sabotage your progress. In the end, you'll wind up with nothing except sad tales and bad memories.

All of these disappointments can be avoided by keeping the following concept in mind: no one wants to be separated from his or her possessions. Be it precious metals, cash, real estate, durable goods, consumable items, or a combination of all of the above, the majority of people who own them worked hard to acquire them and want to keep them.

Simply put, successful people depend on their wealth for their livelihood. Their possessions provide security, comfort, health, wealth, prestige, and more. Consequently, they're normally not in the mood to surrender them unless the price is right, meaning, they must be justly compensated.

Legally, there is only one way to attain the wealth you desire. And that is by "earning it." That means, you must provide something of equal or greater value in exchange for what you want. This type of exchange is usually referred to as a "win-win situation," an arrangement whereby each person gets the things desired from the deal. In some cases, these transactions may require cash, items, labor or legal exchanges.

Any other way of accumulating wealth remains questionable. Some people try to shorten the process by taking drastic actions by cheating, stealing, gambling, hurting others, and even killing those who possess wealth. Obviously, none of these methods are effective means. As a result, those who become successful through these channels will eventually pay the price for their dishonesty.

As one who wants to acquire wealth, you stand on the edge of the world looking in. At that point, no one is particularly thrilled to simply give you what you desire. The supermarket wants cash for the food you need as well as the builder who is ready to sell you the house.

There is also another critical area of interest—the job. The person who occupies your next job isn't ready to move and leave the door open for you before finding something better. So you'll have to wait or go somewhere else.

So, your strategy for financial success should be well planned, one insisting on *improving* the state of others just as much as your own. In other words, you'll get what you want only after satisfying someone else's needs. Only then can you consummate a favorable transaction. Cheating your way through, for instance, will ultimately bother your conscience and turn your wealth into a superficial nightmare. A legitimate transaction, on the other hand, creates a "win-win" environment where both parties walk away feeling satisfied.

The "You First" Concept

It's been said that "no man is an island," a statement that will ring true for eternity. We need one another for emotional and psychological balance. Human-to-human contact minimizes the possibility of running into loneliness, a mental condition prone to depression, insanity, and unusual behavior.

But more than the psychological and emotional stimulation, we need one another for economic reasons as well. Our economy has gotten increasingly complex. As such, it's difficult to get things done without other people's contributions. For instance, all the commodities we use and, sometimes take for granted, are built by others.

Furthermore, the economic system cannot function properly without teachers, clerks, telephone operators, law-enforcement people, automobile technicians, data-entry personnel, and the list goes on. Therefore, everyone around us is important including our friends, neighbors, and relatives.

However, as benevolent as our relationship is to one another, our focus is not on those who work with us. We're motivated purely by self-centeredness. Our first and primary concern is survival. Thus, at the base of our cooperative effort is our *self-interest.*

For some people, this concept could be hard to swallow and, as a result, may take offense to it. But no matter how they look at it, few people can argue the fact that our individual desire to fulfill our needs comes first. And it's from our personal passion to live comfortably, securely, and happily that we find the motivation to work.

For some, this outlook on life may appear to be selfish because they can't imagine doing anything for personal benefit. But "What's in it for me?" is nothing new, even though Generation X may try to claim that phrase. But more specifically, self-motivation (spoken or unspoken) is the driving force behind everything we do.

Again, if you find yourself on the opposite side of this issue, I'm not surprised. The reality is that for years we've been taught to believe that "self-interest" is a *negative* concept, one represented by greed and selfishness. This view on life focuses chiefly on oneself while disregarding the needs and interest of others. On the other hand, "selflessness" is a *positive* gesture, an attitude that denies self while seeing to the needs of others.

Viewed in this fashion, it's not hard to take sides. Frankly, everyone wants to be seen in a good light, particularly a condition in which one is observed meeting the needs of others while sacrificing his or her own. Conversely, no one wants to appear to be a scrooge, a villain, or a user of others. This attitude is offensive, distasteful, and cruel.

In light of this, you certainly have the choice to believe what you want. Nevertheless, you also need to be told that as long as you continue to live, you'll instinctively do whatever is necessary to stay alive. That includes employing your natural ability to finding food, shelter, clothing, and anything else deemed necessary to stay comfortable, healthy, safe, and secure.

Unfortunately, this approach to life isn't very appealing because it exposes the unrefined or raw nature of man, thus, making some people who appear to be compassionate, loving, and kind very uncomfortable. These people work hard to hide their self-interest as they go through life doing good. Therefore, any statement suggesting self-centeredness appalls them.

Their reaction is understandable. But don't be fooled. All of us have a reason for getting into the action. While the gain or benefit may not always be money, it could be something just as valuable such as a simple pat on the back, praise, name recognition, or appreciation. For some, these compliments mean more than money itself. So on one hand, while many of us try *not* to appear self-centered, our actions won't let us get away with it. Our true motive gets revealed at the most critical moment.

The good news is, regardless what the culture suggests, admitting to self-centeredness is perfectly normal and safe. It's a natural response to life that needs no apologies. Yet those who deny being self-centered are simply kidding themselves. For example, no one goes into business just because he or she loves the idea of dealing with customer complaints, employee headaches, Occupational Safety and Health Administration (OSHA) regulations, and the Internal Revenue Service harassments. Neither do you, or anyone else for that matter, wake up each morning for work, desiring to increase the boss's bottom line.

Instead, each day, we wake up to do anything we do with the intent of improving ourselves. Then, as we focus on our needs, others get blessed in the process. Once this becomes clear, life takes on a fresh, new meaning. Suddenly, you begin to see everyone at work unabashedly doing what must be done to survive.

On the other hand, you may have noticed that staying focused on your personal needs is not always easy. Periodic distractions have a tendency to throw us out of alignment. For instance, concern for others, particularly relatives, is one of the biggest distractions to wealth building. Sometimes, when relatives impose on us with their personal needs, we get flustered and disoriented. When that happens, the ripple effect may last a lifetime, causing us to achieve less in life than we would otherwise.

I speak specifically of financial independence. Since money is the means by which we solve most of our problems, it seems like every situation within a family circle needing assistance requires cash, a limited commodity in most homes, including yours. Therefore, the handling of such a situation requires financial wisdom because as you attempt to resolve one problem, you could be jeopardizing your own, creating two separate casualties at the same time.

This happens all time. Not too long ago, I answered a desperate call from a client. "How badly will a voluntary car repossession affect my job and credit report?" the gentleman asked. I asked him, "Why are you considering this move?"

"I'm two months late on my car payments, and the rest of my bills are falling behind. I'm struggling to regain control, but I simply can't make it." "What caused this situation?" I asked.

"Well," he replied, "recently, my mother needed some financial help, and we assisted her. However, in the process of providing help, we ended up giving her more money than we could afford."

No question about it, this couple was backed up against the wall. Not only did they become a casualty, too, but it's also doubtful that they were able to help his mother completely. Usually, these types of rescues require a lot of ongoing financial resources, which, in most cases, are hard to come by. The truth is, most of us have a limited sum of money, making it hard to sustain our situation while assisting others for any lengthy period. Such may have been the case here.

As I think about the financial plight of the baby boomers, I see the same thing. This group went through the most productive years of their lives, spending and borrowing. Then during their forties, they woke up to realize that they barely had any cash or other types of assets for financial stability. As a result, in the last twenty-five years, many of them have been scrambling to accumulate wealth.

Regrettably, as they attempt to make some financial progress, they consistently run into roadblocks. Realistically, their financial resources have been exposed to "triple dipping." In addition to maintaining their immediate household needs, they're also stuck with the responsibility of sending children to college while providing for aging parents. Hence, the phrase *sandwich generation.* The term conveys the idea that this group is being squeezed in the middle by outside forces, in this case, meeting the financial needs of children as well as parents.

Today, the boomers are the busiest people in our country. Roughly 70 million of us are burning the candle at both ends hoping to stay afloat. Meanwhile, millions of us are complaining about physical, emotional, and psychological exhaustion. In short, we're burned-out. And although most of us would like to slow down or walk away from the rat race, we can't afford to do so. We're caught in the wilderness of debt and can't seem to find our way back. Sadly, our children have been following our trails all along, and they are making the same mistakes.

I'm not suggesting that you shouldn't help those in need, particularly those who are closest to you. The recommendation here is to exercise *prudence.*

The "you first" concept suggests that you take time to stabilize your situation first. It's only after you're strong and able that you can provide assistance. Doing it any other way is asking for trouble. For example, if you're hungry, it's hard to feed others; if you don't have a home, it's hard to provide shelter to those who need it; and if you're in peril of any type, it's difficult to bring others to safety.

Furthermore, "the blind cannot lead the blind." Neither can the poor help the poor. If you disregard this concept, you will become financial casualties again and again.

CHAPTER 14

Two Noteworthy Attributes of Money

In the school of business management, students are made to understand that every earthly resource is limited, not only in terms of longevity, but also in terms of scope. The lives of animals, plants, and even people have a beginning and an ending. And once our allotted time has expired, we all eventually disappear into the unknown, never to be seen again.

This concept embraces a wider scope, however. In addition to animal lives, it encompasses everything else in the universe, including natural and manmade. The land and water around us, for example, are limited to what we see. So is all the sand on the beaches of the world.

An understanding of limits in our universe is crucial for success in any endeavor because once precious resources are depleted, it's difficult to replace them. Lower and midlevel managers who are aware of the concept of limits are usually paid handsomely for their commitment. They're generally referred to as *guardians of resources* because of their ability to preserve what they've been given. For example, in the event that a tree is cut down for lumber, five or ten small ones are planted as replacements. Furthermore, employees (the most valuable resources in a company) are treated as humans as opposed to commodities.

Conversely, managers with no regard to limits have a different outlook on life. They squander their entrusted supplies, thinking that there is always more available for them. So they habitually create an environment of insufficiency, one that continually expects more, but is never satisfied.

The concept of limits is the same when dealing with money. You, as a manager of your own finances, need to not only understand it, but to also apply it.

The Limits of Money

On a practical level, we're aware of the fact that money is a limited commodity. We're reminded of this daily when our pocketbooks and bank accounts go dry. On a psychological level, however, we behave as though our money supply will never run out. This behavior becomes quite obvious as we consistently commit our limited income to ceaseless spending.

It is within this paradox that we reexamine the concept of limits. Somehow, we need to be reminded periodically that money, particularly income, is a measured commodity. For instance, all the revenue the government collects in taxes each year is limited to that amount. Corporate sales or service revenue is limited to the amount collected in a given quarter or year. And people's salaries or wages are also measured by the size of their paychecks.

For the most part, this makes perfect sense to us on an intelligent level. For example, we can assume that the government is aware of the amount of money it collects in taxes. Most people can tell the balance in their checking and savings accounts. The same could be said about the money we receive in salary or wages. Operating within the boundaries of these limits, however, is something altogether different. In fact, this is one of our biggest challenges. We have a hard time living or conducting business within our financial scope.

Take the government, for example. Each year, lawmakers pass a budget based on anticipated revenue from taxes. Once the budget is approved and taxes are collected, various portions of money goes to each active department within the government. Then, it's the responsibility of each department head to operate within the limits of their allotted portion. Most often, the departments run out of money due to excessive spending. Consequently, each year, lawmakers face the same challenge of having to raise taxes for yet a larger budget.

Corporations and small businesses experience the same limits in revenue. The only difference is that these groups retain tighter control over their budgets because unlike the government that can raise taxes at random for runaway spending, private companies have little control over the money they make. The amount of revenue they generate is subject to all the external control of providing a commodity or service to the public. Consequently, for a small business to survive, spending must be kept under control.

Private citizens should be just as sensitive about their financial issues because the operation of a home is no different from running a traditional business. In fact, no matter how you look at it, every American home is a complete economic system of its own. Here is a parallel worth noting: A regular enterprise sells *goods* or *services* to generate revenue. A home requires working adults to sell their *time* to generate income. One minor difference is this: Money in a business is referred to as "revenue." In the home, it's referred to as income, salary, or wages. Yet the same dollar flows through the government, large corporations, small business, and even other homes. In other words, all entities (home, business, and government) function within the same economic concept. The same financial accounting system applies to all of them equally.

The unfortunate aspect of home economics is that too many Americans don't think in terms of business as they operate the home. That explains why the majority of us don't use budgets. We think about it, talk about it, encourage others to use it, yet few of us apply it. It's as though we understand the value of a budget to be a good thing. Yet the application is not that important in our private lives. For millions of us, a budget is nothing more than a conversation piece.

But how can one fully understand the limits of money without a budget? Financial management begins to make sense only when seen on paper. It is truly from this point of view you that can see the limits of income and expenses. Disregarding this written aspect of your finances is like walking in darkness. You will eventually end up in a ditch, hurting yourself in the process.

It's not surprising, then, to realize that roughly 90 percent of the homes in this country struggle with financial issues. More than 1.5 million Americans file bankruptcy each year, and the rest of us are either seeking debt-consolidation solutions or barely holding on by our fingernails. The truth is, we consistently run over the boundaries of our income, by living above our means.

We love to chastise public entities for bad financial performance. We criticize companies for laying off employees or filing bankruptcy as a result of poor financial management. We rebuke the government and political leaders for mismanaging and squandering taxpayers' money.

At the same time, we tend to overlook our own financial debacle as though we should be held blameless for our behavior. But not so fast. Daily, the evidence of our financial ignorance is seen by our own financial folly. In other words, "the proof is in the pudding." Our personal, financial track record is proof enough to show that the limits of money is a mute point in our financial affairs.

Yet a lot of our financial problems can be minimized or eliminated by applying the concept of limits to our funds. The reality is, whether you make $30,000 or $600,000 income a year, that portion of money is limited to this amount—no more, no less. How you manage it depends on how well you discipline yourself on spending.

To do this properly, you need a spending plan. That means, creating boundaries around every expenditure item before you get your pay (see table 14.1).

Table 14.1 (Annual Spending Plan)						
DESCRIPTION	Jan 05	Feb 05	Mar 05	Apr 05	May 05	Jun 05
INCOME ($60,000 gross per yr)	$5,000	$5,000	$5,000	$5,000	$5,000	$5,000
EXPENSE						
Housing	$1600	$1600	$1600	$1600	$1600	$1600
Personal savings	$300	$300	$300	$300	$300	$300
Transportation	$700	$700	$700	$700	$700	$700
Food	$750	$750	$750	$750	$750	$750
Entertainment	$250	$250	$250	$250	$250	$250
Personal taxes	$450	$450	$450	$450	$450	$450
Health care	$250	$250	$250	$250	$250	$250
Clothing	$200	$200	$200	$200	$200	$200
Cash Contribution	$100	$100	$100	$100	$100	$100
Miscellaneous	$100	$100	$100	$100	$100	$100
Balance/ Difference (-/+)	$300	$300	$300	$300	$300	$300

As you can tell, this model is somewhat fictitious. Nevertheless, it gets the point across. The idea is to put on paper the measured amount of income and expenses you anticipate within a given period. This way, you can see exactly what's taking place with your finances.

At the very least, every American household needs a model like this one. In this sample, the numbers are stretched to six months. However, it's highly encouraged to cover a period of twelve months at a time, giving you the kind of financial perspective you need for a year.

Keep in mind that this spending plan is only half the work necessary for good financial management. Realistically, numbers on paper, like this model, can do only so much. The other portion of this exercise is to implement personal control or financial discipline in your life—much of which should take place while shopping. That means walking away from sudden urges to spend money impulsively. It also means realizing that once your cash is spent, your buying should stop.

Unless you discipline yourself in this fashion, the numbers in your budget will have little meaning. In other words, if you continue shopping beyond your income boundary, you're potentially creating a financial quagmire that will come back to haunt you.

The Mystifying Nature of Money

"Now you see me, and now you don't." This saying is most popular among children while playing games. Yet it could be just as appropriate in the world of finance. Money, it seems, has perfected the art of vanishing without a trace, a mystifying ploy that has stunned millions of people through the ages.

Call it fiction, magic, witchcraft, or any other puzzling impression, the feeling is universal. Over the years, people have made statements like, "Money flies," implying that money has the ability to grow wings and fly away at will, or, "Money is burning holes in my pocket," again suggesting that money is restless and wants to be let loose. "I don't know where my money went," is another common phrase people have used, signifying a lack of personal control over the commodity.

Based on these comments, it seems that money has its own personality but, unlike people, its behavior is predictable, making it easy to control. Still, it appears that a lot of people have difficulty controlling it. The obvious question is, *"Why?"* Well, it seems that money should be treated one way as opposed to another. Those who have taken the time to find out how money should be cared for are the same people who are highly successful today.

This situation needs no further explanation except to say that money essentially occupies one of two positions in our lives: *master* or *slave*. For those who have the knowledge, skill, and experience to manage money well, it becomes their *slave* or *servant*. It listens to them and cooperates with their plans for success. As such, money works diligently night and day, multiplying itself through the concept of compounding interest. In this case, you could say that money is extremely happy because it gets the opportunity to do what it loves best—to build wealth for those who manage it well.

This scenario gives meaning to the phrase that many of us have come to dislike, which is, "The rich keep getting richer." In many ways, this is true. Simply, those who have developed the discipline to put money away in the bank or in other types of investments will continue to grow wealthy. The idea is no more complicated than that. And those who understand this concept and make an effort to accumulate enough money to lend to others will keep their wealth growing.

Those, on the other hand, who lack the ability to manage money well will always struggle financially. In this relationship, money becomes their illusive *master*. It controls them instead of them controlling it. Money limits its exposure to abusive characters such as impulsive spenders and financially illiterate people. Furthermore, money flees from people who waste it, steal it, gamble it, and smoke it. It takes wings and flies away from their control, leaving them wondering what happened.

These wasters will continually struggle to make ends meet. Because of their abusive personality, they never seem to get enough money to conduct business. Yet within their environment exists a constant yearning for extra money. One can visualize people exhaustively chasing the dollar for the rest of their lives (see figure 14.2) For many, that means holding two and three jobs at a time, trying to survive. In this case, money is definitely in control. It leads, and they follow.

Fig. 14.2

This type of upside-down relationship exists because we've come to believe that the only way to keep making money is by chasing it through hard labor. As such, we deny money the opportunity to work for us. Instead, we work for it.

For example, those of us who don't save or invest money (regardless how small the amount) in some type of lucrative endeavor will never get the chance to see how well money can create extra money. The same is true for those who try to save or invest but quickly ravage their small investment prematurely for impulsive, spending urges.

Given the chance, money has the capacity to grow fast. It starts as a small seedling and quickly turns into a mammoth tree over time. But one has to give it the opportunity to do so. Unfortunately, most of us don't give it the chance to develop. We use it too quickly. With this habit, it's not hard to see how the poor keep getting poorer. Most of the time, they simply sabotage their own success, wondering why it's so difficult to become wealthy.

For you, however, the situation is going to change as a result of this newfound knowledge. Starting today, you're going to allow money to be your slave instead of your master. You're going to (1) gain more knowledge about its potential, (2) exercise personal discipline when shopping, (3) avoid abusing the commodity, (4) respect its property, and (5) allow it the opportunity to do what it loves to do best: to increase in value.

CHAPTER 15

The Five Functions of Money

For those with limited financial knowledge, money management is restricted to two basic functions: *income* and *expenses*. As far as they're concerned, money comes *in* as income and *leaves* as expenses. In this situation, money is nothing more than a commodity that's passing through to accomplish a desired end. So once the food, rent, and other basic commodities are purchased, the purpose of money is over, at least that's what they think. But indeed, this is a short-term view of money.

If everyone viewed money this way, life would be different as we know it. Not only would the financial cycle be incomplete but people would be less hopeful about the future. For instance, professional growth would be stunted, people's movements would be more confined or restricted, we would have less incentive to dream, the economy would crawl at a slower pace, and the future would hold less promises for those who aspire greatness.

Fortunately, people with financial knowledge see money as a commodity with a wider reach. They see a bigger picture. To them, money has five separate and distinct functions, all of which come together to form a complete financial cycle. Yet each depends on the other for financial balance. When one is used, the others are affected equally—positively or negatively. As such, one of the keys to financial success is knowing how to effectively use the five functions of money for maximum financial leverage.

Figure 15.1 is a diagram I refer to as *The Financial Chessboard*. This diagram is designed to acquaint you with the various functions of money.

If you happen to know these functions well, the model may appear simple. Nonetheless, there are millions of people who are unfamiliar with the natural flow of money. For them, this model will make it easy to demonstrate the financial activities that take place in our lives every day.

In this chapter, the model is presented as an introduction only. The purpose is to briefly describe the five individual segments of money and allow room in the next chapter for practical application in the American culture.

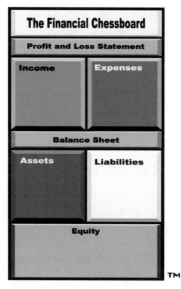

Fig. 15.1

As shown, *The Financial Chessboard* has five major sections—*income, expenses, liabilities, assets,* and *equity*—all of which are more or less self-explanatory. The model is given this name because it has some of the characteristics of a chessboard, in which case, your money is seen as the chess pieces. The aim, here, is to start visualizing the world of money as a massive chess game, and you're one of the *volunteer* players.

Notice the word *volunteer,* a term suggesting a personal willingness to participate in a given situation. In this case, it's a financial game. The concept is, the day you started earning money, you automatically placed yourself in the economic chess game. The fact that you may or may not have known the rules of the game made no difference. You're being treated as equals, assuming you know what you're doing.

Each time you handle money in the economy, you're actually moving the commodity from one square of the chessboard to the next. Meanwhile, your opponent (everyone else in the game) is watching your moves, hoping to capitalize on your weakness, your limited financial knowledge or discipline.

The interesting thing is, it makes no difference whose money you're managing. You could, in fact, be operating the federal or state budget, the finances of a large corporation, the funds of a small business, or your personal finances. In each case, the volume of money would probably be different. Nonetheless, the rules of *The Financial Chessboard* affects each portion of money the same way.

Therefore, as a player, depending on which square you place your most valued piece (the various portions of your funds) determines whether you'll win or lose the financial game. As such, it makes sense to understand the rules of the game prior to playing, that is, if you desire to win.

Income: The First Function of Money

For most people, the meaning of *income* is the money earned through one source: the job (see figure 15.2).

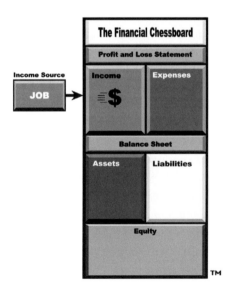

Fig. 15.2

Nevertheless, income covers a broader meaning than the immediate paycheck. Realistically, it includes not only wages or salary but also profits, tips, interests, gifts, and so on.

It also means more than simply receiving a direct deposit into your checking account each payday. This element of finance is the root of our economic system. Without it, the world of business would be absolutely meaningless. Government and business operations would be functionally ineffective, and personal dreams would remain hopelessly dangling. In other words, everything starts and stops with income.

Expenses: The Second Function of Money

Expenses, as you know, depict the *outflow* of income. When money comes in as income, it needs an outlet. *The Financial Chessboard* uses the expense square as the outlet for cash. From there, it ends up in what I call *the economic black hole* (see figure 15.3).

This process of *cash in, cash out* is the two-step method mentioned earlier. Money comes in as income and leaves as expenses. When it leaves, it's usually used for *needs* and *wants*. So in reality, money simply passes from one section of the diagram to the next, or from one person to the next.

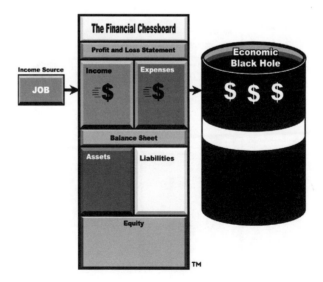

Fig. 15.3

Unfortunately, this two-step process is an incomplete money-management scheme. It provides little or no financial security for the future except basic survival needs. Yet as far as millions of Americans are concerned, that's the extent of their financial management plan, a scheme that's desperately lacking balance and common sense.

Liabilities: The Third Function of Money

As previously cited, the majority of Americans have no trouble understanding the meaning of income and expenses. These terms are common household words that get tossed around every day as we go about conducting business.

However, the term *liability* puts a different twist on things. Many people associate the name only with business enterprises. For them, only accountants, bookkeepers, managers, and chief executive officers (CEOs) deal with liabilities.

But how wrong can they be? A liability is one of the basic functions of money regardless of where the money is used. And that's especially true for the home. For instance, anyone who has purchased a car, house, furniture, etc., on credit has incurred a liability. And when that happens, a portion of money must flow from the income square into the liability square (see figure 15.4).

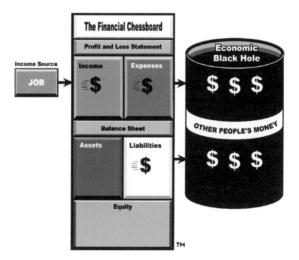

Fig. 15.4

The money that flows into the liability section of the diagram ultimately makes its way to the outside world never to be seen again.

Assets: The Fourth Function of Money

The asset square on *The Financial Chessboard* represents a positive aspect of your financial picture. The content could be hard assets such as business properties or liquid assets such as cash investments. Sometimes, it's a combination of both. Notice that the dollar sign in figure 15.5 flows upward.

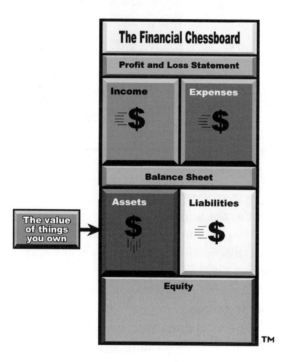

Fig. 15.5

Equity: The Fifth Function of Money

The equity section of *The Financial Chessboard* is your achievement report card (see figure 15.6).

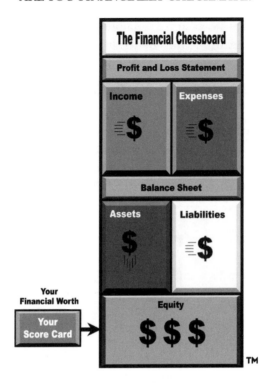

Fig. 15.6

It represents the net difference between your assets and liabilities and provides a real picture of your financial position. In accounting language, the net difference is referred to as "net worth," the limit of your total wealth.

It could be that you've never thought of money in this fashion. You simply went about your daily routine of making money and spending it. The interesting thing is, whether you've been using all of these money functions or not, they have been influencing your financial outcome. And realistically, they'll continue to do so.

In Chapter 16, we'll explore the details of *The Financial Chessboard*. We'll examine how every American home, including yours, is being affected by the five functions of money. In the process, you'll learn how to avoid the financial or economic mistakes that keep most people broke.

CHAPTER 16

Money in Action

In Chapter 15, we mentioned the fact that the economy (the place of business in our culture) is like a giant chessboard, and the money we use represents the chess pieces: pawns, bishops, knights, rooks, queens, and kings. As we go about conducting our financial affairs, we're simply moving dollars and cents from one square of the board to the next as one would do in a chess game.

As players, we all anticipate winning the financial game. We want to experience the freedom, power, and control that money brings. So we use a variety of methods in order to achieve this goal. In addition to attaining an education, some of us stretch the dollar to make it last as long as possible. Some of us extend our working hours. Others hold two and three jobs at a time. Some of us are very frugal, anticipating the collection of as much money as possible. Many of us invest in the stock market, hoping to strike it rich. And rest of us don't care one way or the other.

As you can tell, the way we approach the financial game differs from one individual to another. Yet, we want the same results—to become financially independent. But like the chess game, you must take time to learn the rules of money (financial knowledge) and develop some working strategies to win the game. In other words, if you want to be financially independent, you can't spend time learning yoga, history, photography, and a host of other unrelated topics and hope to be rich. Granted, you may get the opportunity to make some money as a result of your talent. But if you don't know how to manage it well, your wealth won't last very long.

And so it is, while you hope to become financially independent, your limited money-management skills put you at a sharp disadvantage with people who know how money works. And since your opponents know the rules of the game, they'll keep winning again and again, leaving you and most Americans wondering what's wrong.

Today, we know that roughly 90 percent of the people in this country are working hard to make ends meet. And the remaining 10 percent control most of the wealth in the United States. Some of us may argue that the smaller segment of the population has unique talents, giving them an edge over the rest of us. Otherwise, they are extremely lucky and the rest of us are ill-fated.

Say what you wish, but most of these individuals started out as average Americans. That is, in spite of what you've heard over the years about the rich, wealth wasn't simply handed to them. Less than 1 percent of this group has actually inherited wealth. Moreover, fewer have won the lottery. And when they do, much of the money goes up in smoke within three to five years. Wealthy Americans have accumulated their riches through proven concepts, financial knowledge (rules of the game) that have worked well for people who have taken the time to learn them.

In this chapter and the following one, we'll actually track the flow of money, showing you how one can become financially successful. Your job, as one who wants to be financially free, is to observe some of the money-management patterns of the rich and those of average Americans while playing the financial chess game. By doing so, you'll not only learn how to avoid the financial pitfalls of most Americans, but you'll also learn how to develop your own strategies for financial independence.

The Financial Chessboard

By now, you should be well familiar with the various sections of *The Financial Chessboard*. The diagram is basically straightforward in its approach as it depicts terms that are well known. What we haven't covered thoroughly is the way money moves within the system and how it affects you as it happens. To begin, the diagram represents a simplified version of the accounting process. Yet it avoids some of the complexities associated with accounting, none of which are essential here. The point is to depict the flow of money and examine its outcome as it changes from one classification to another.

Keep in mind that each of us is a player. If you're generating any type of income, you have your own accounting system: *The Financial Chessboard*. The advantage here is that you'll be able to see how others play their games and compare your moves to theirs. Ultimately, your job is to make sure that money flows in the block or direction that provides you maximum leverage.

To start, notice that the board is divided into two main sections: a profit-and-loss statement including *income* and *expenses* and a balance sheet including *assets, liabilities, and equity* (see figure 16.1).

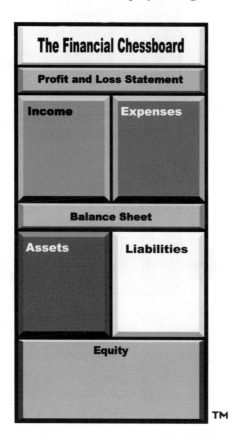

Fig. 16.1

These various components make up your entire accounting system, providing you with a comprehensive view of your financial situation.

There are two more points about the diagram that are important: Notice that the right side of the board is negative, and the left side is positive (see figure 16.2).

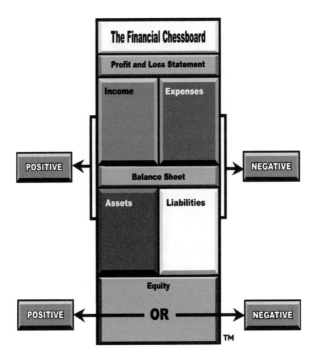

Fig. 16.2

Also, notice that the bottom section could be either negative or positive. So comprehensively, this board is uniquely shaped to provide *instant portability,* meaning, once you understand the concept, it can be mentally transported to any business situation. The idea is, whenever you deal with money, you should be able to tell instantly whether you're making a winning or losing move, giving you immediate feedback for control.

Money In

Money in needs no elaborate explanation. It represents the income we get through various means, e.g., jobs, profits, interest on security investments, etc. In Chapter 15, we said that this part of money is the most vital component of our economic system. Without an adequate supply of it, unpleasant things happen. For instance, businesses fail or go bankrupt, people stay broke, dreams remain unfulfilled, and others go hungry.

So an adequate supply of income is unequivocally essential for a comfortable lifestyle. Consequently, your income must be able to stand the test of time no matter what happens to the economy.

Therefore, as a wage earner, one of your responsibilities is to learn how to secure your financial base. One of the best ways to do this is by gradually removing your dependency from one source of income, regardless of how reliable it may appear to be, while developing two or more income streams.

For you, this approach to financial security may be a new thing. And if that's the case, it may appear to be risky. However, people who understand the power in this concept have been capitalizing on it for years, thus, creating huge amounts of wealth in the process.

The average American, on the other hand, has been taught to rely on only one source of income: the job (see figure 16.3).

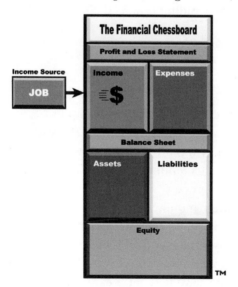

Fig. 16.3

The reason is that over the years, we've been influenced by the culture to think that the job is the most reliable and secure source of income.

For all we know, that may have been the case at one point. But that's no longer true. Lately, millions of us have come to realize that wages from jobs are anything but secure and reliable.

Layoffs have created havoc in people's lives. Yet, there is no end to unemployment or worker displacement. The proof is in the headlines we see and hear everyday, For instance, in addition to the scaling back of employees by the airlines and other industries, the government is in the process of replacing long-term workers with private contracts. Also, corporations are now looking overseas for cheaper labor to meet the high-tech demand in this country, a situation that puts an untold number of workers at risk of losing their income.

Obviously, this type of news doesn't necessarily rest well with those who feel vulnerable. People have a tendency to become extremely nervous at the thought of losing their jobs or income.

But isn't that the point? Anyone who depends on one source of income is potentially threatened in an unpredictable economy such as ours. This is why an individual should find ways to develop additional revenue sources, in a good economy when everything appears to be doing well, thereby avoiding financial chaos in a downswing economic situation.

Money Out

Money out represents expenses. In Chapter 14, we talked about the fact that money has its own characteristics. In addition to its color, size, and denomination, it has a mind of its own. One of the most notable features of money is its tendency to travel. By doing so, it creates additional money in the process.

Therefore, when money comes to us in the form of *income,* it's simply passing through. As such, it does not to stay or loiter without a purpose. Money loses value and feels useless as people handle it without a plan. So when you receive your paycheck, the idea is to use it to your advantage while you have it. That means, placing it in the appropriate square on your financial chessboard, assuming you know the right one.

Unfortunately, this is where most of us begin to lose control of money. Since the majority of us lack sound financial know-how, we make repeated and costly mistakes year after year. We have no problem making money but capitalizing on its strength is one of our biggest challenges.

As soon as we get money in hand, we instantly feel compelled to spend it. Accordingly, we end up making careless and unreasonable purchasing decisions.

Escape through Expenses

One of the ways money gets away from us, of course, is through regular *expenses*—the money we spend for every day *needs* and *wants*. For example, assume your household income ranges between $2,500 and $10,000 a month (see figure 16.4).

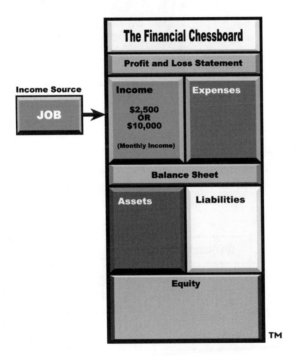

Fig. 16.4

That's the extent of your income, in which case, the only difference between you and one who earns more or less money is your lifestyle. In other words, your level of income will place you in your own socio-economic class. There, you should be able to pay for all your basic needs as shown in the expense section of figure 16.5.

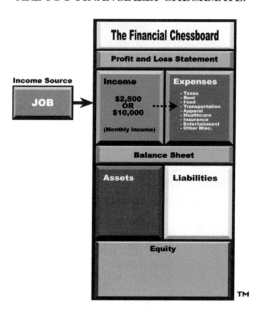

Fig. 16.5

But be cautious. Regardless of how much money you bring home, if you allow all of it to slip through your fingers while shopping and, ultimately, end up in *the economic black hole,* you've lost control (see figure 16.6).

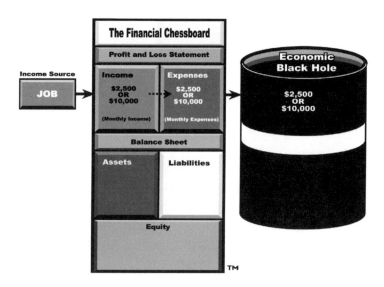

Fig. 16.6

This is one of the ways money may escape you without you noticing its departure. Unfortunately, this type of thing happens when we attempt to buy more than we can afford to pay.

By the way, this is a classic case of *economic engulfing,* a condition in which the economy provides you an income but takes 100 percent back from you. In the language of business, it would be said that you're breaking even—making $1 and spending $1.

With this kind of situation, you could be tricked into thinking that you're making financial progress. But are you? The answer is obviously "no." In a break even situation you're neither winning nor losing. In this case, you're simply surviving to pay bills. In other words, all of your income or cash ends up in the hands of the landlord, the grocer, the utility people, the auto finance company, and so forth. Regrettably, when this happens, this part of your income is gone forever. And if you're not careful, this pattern could go on for months and even years.

Notwithstanding, you deserve a commendation. Although your personal financial progress is negligible, you're at least breaking even. You're, in fact, staying within the boundary of your income, which is a difficult thing to do these days. Culturally, we're being bombarded each day to buy, buy, buy, and it takes a strong will to resist the temptation and stay within budget. So be proud of your success in that sense because it could be worse.

The bottom line is that you must put yourself in a position where you're spending less than you make. This makes sense regardless of your income level. With the foregoing spending habit, one with $600,000 income a year could stay just as broke as one with $60,000.

Escape through Liabilities

The other way money gets away from us is through *liabilities* or debt obligations. Mind you, this is where most Americans get *financially checkmate* or immobilized. Culturally, we're led to believe that we're making progress in life when we purchase big-ticket items such as houses and cars on credit when, in fact, the lifestyle we create through liabilities is nothing more than an illusion.

Liabilities occur in three ways: (1) when people's cash is completely spent and then continue to shop with borrowed money; (2) when one chooses to buy an expensive item such as a house and has limited cash on hand to do so; (3) when a person chooses to keep some cash on hand and borrows extra money for financial leverage. In all of cases, credit is used to create the debt or *liability*.

In this culture, just about everyone has liabilities. Companies borrow money from banks to buy plants, equipment, and materials; the government borrows money from private citizens in exchange for bonds; and individual Americans take out personal loans, car loans, mortgage loans, and cash advances on credit cards. In short, without the use of liabilities, our lifestyles would be different. Most of us simply don't make enough money to pay cash for large ticket items like houses. Consequently, credit becomes the only means by which most of us pay for them.

But with the privilege of using credit also comes certain risks. Major problems arise as a result of overspending. Let's assume that you're breaking even with your finances. That means, you've depleted your cash, and you have stopped shopping. At this point, it could be that you're being tempted to borrow additional money to buy some of the things you crave. The moment you borrow the extra money, you've crossed over your income limit and walked directly into the liability or debt category.

When this happens, you must exercise caution. As mentioned before, as a group, we consistently spend roughly $1.20 to every $1.00 we take home, a habit that keeps the majority of us in an endless cycle of borrowing (see figure 16.7). Sadly, this is the same situation that keeps us broke.

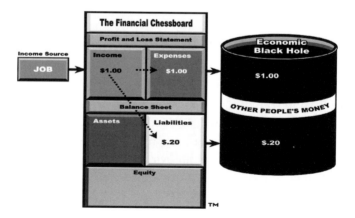

Fig. 16.7

If your financial picture looks like this, you may not realize that you're sliding backward. In fact, you may get the feeling that you're making progress, that is, until you face the truth. For example, assume that your combined household income is $7,500 a month. Based on a national average, your monthly expenditures may look like this (see figure 16.8).

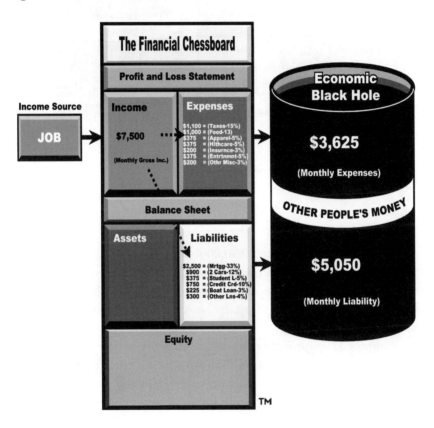

Fig. 16.8

Notice that the bulk of your income is going toward debts. Take a look at figure 16.9.

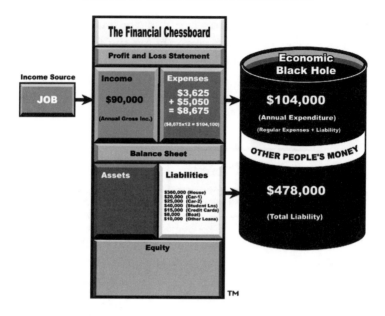

Fig. 16.9

Your gross annual income is $90,000, and your annual expenditures (regular *expenses* plus *liabilities*) amount to $104,000, exceeding your income by roughly 16 percent. Additionally, your total liability amounts to $478,000, your house weighing the heaviest: 75 percent of your total liability.

In Chapter 12, your were made aware that the majority of us spend more money on houses and cars than we can afford. We do so partly because the culture promotes home ownership as the path to ultimate success. The idea is conveyed to the public that until Americans make the effort to buy a house, they'll never be successful.

However, the home-buying message is not entirely forthcoming. In fact, it's somewhat deceptive, particularly to those who depend on the wisdom of real-estate agents, brokers, and bankers to make sensible financial decisions.

As mentioned earlier, buying a house doesn't necessarily mean that one is making a good financial choice. Neither does it mean that he or she is attaining financial success. Yet prospective home buyers are being duped into believing that once they purchase a house that they're automatically building wealth. Instead, they're piling on *liability*, a path that's plagued with potential economic risks. Unfortunately, few of us see the problems associated with "home ownership," even while experiencing financial difficulty in maintaining a house.

A Grim Lesson in Home Ownership

As I write this section, my home-ownership experience surfaces. After years of moving from one apartment to the next, it was a thrill to finally settle in a brand new house: a small three-bedroom, two-bath single family dwelling. The whole family loved the house because it was attractive, convenient, and comfortable.

However, it took some doing to bring the house up to acceptable standards. After moving in, we did what most proud American homeowners would do. We upgraded the carpet, installed wallpaper, improved the landscape, built a patio and walkway, and built additional storage spaces. Furthermore, I attended all homeowners' association meetings, kept up with local property ordinances, paid all taxes and association fees, and never missed a mortgage payment in eight years.

Then, my employment situation changed. I lost my job in a tough economy and had to settle for a $6 an hour job. Scrambling to hold things together, I notified the lien holder (bank) about my situation. At first, it appeared that the bank understood my dilemma and was willing to cooperate with me until things got better.

After missing one mortgage payment, the bank reminded me of it and tacked on late charges to the amount due. I wrote back, describing my ongoing effort to find reliable employment, and requested additional consideration. But as time passed, things went from bad to worse. Three months into the ordeal, the bank started foreclosure proceedings on the house.

To say the least, I was shocked and heartbroken. I was about to be evicted from the property, and the house that had become my home was about to be taken from me and given to someone else. As far as the bank was concerned, since I had defaulted on the contract, I had no more rights to the property. The situation could probably change if I could bring the account current. That meant paying all back payments including late fees.

It was then I became acutely aware of the immense power and control of a lien holder. Frankly, when it came right down to business, the crude reality was that neither the bank nor the rest of my creditors cared about my predicament. Suddenly, the eight years of consistent mortgage payments and good credit rating meant nothing. Since I was unable to continue making payments on my *liabilities*, I was about to be discarded by the economic system.

I sobbed for days over my calamity while trying to find a way out of the situation. Although I was able to save the house, I was left with a profound respect for debt or liability. After that experience, I haven't been able to avoid using credit entirely. But all things being equal, I've come to depend on it less and less.

What about your personal situation? Is your house an exception? I think not unless it's paid for in cash. And even then, the Internal Revenue Service (IRS) could dictate your fate should you be delinquent on your taxes.

To start, it needs to be understood that one cannot be in the habit of increasing the negative and hoping to achieve a greater amount of the positive. Life experiences rarely turn out that way, and arithmetic supports this theory as well. Going back to one of our previous models, we see a vivid demonstration of *liability* overload, a condition suggesting that if you desire to build financial security, taking this path is danger-ously risky to your lifestyle (see figure 16.10).

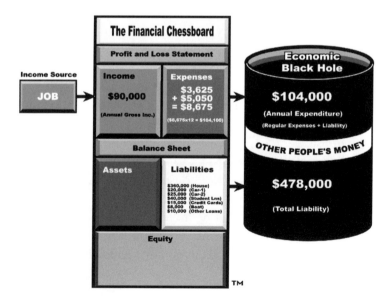

Fig. 16.10

If your personal situation looks anything close to this, you're *financially checkmate* without even realizing it. Take your mortgage, for instance. Your loan amount is $360,000. Assume that your interest rate is 5.75 percent for the next thirty years, you'll end up paying roughly $390,000 in interest, bringing your total mortgage obligation to $750,000 ($360,000 + $390,000), presumably you live in the house for the next thirty years. This sum alone will keep you working for the rest of your life. The worst of it is that you'll end up making this much money and more, but you'll get to keep little or none of it.

Now, from the outside, your situation looks mighty impressive. Yet if one were to peer into your personal situation, the view would be entirely different. Your *liability* obligation is dominating your lifestyle. Since lien holders are involved in all of your major purchases, they own the goods you claim to have—most of your possessions.

Therefore, until you're able to purchase these items outright, you're simply permitted to use them with strings attached. Meanwhile, you're probably straining financially to keep up with monthly payments. Should anything go wrong with your income, all your possessions could simply disappear in the blink of an eye.

While being squeezed financially, it's easy to think that more money will naturally solve your problem. This is a common rationale, especially for people who consistently overspend. These individuals usually lack good financial discipline and money-management skills. As a result, their story has the same ending: more money simply means more headaches. Suppose that you're one of these overspending individuals, and one day you miraculously double your income. At this point, it would make sense to wipe away as much *liability* as quickly as possible. But instead, you will naturally expand your lifestyle like most Americans do. That usually means an increase in liability. Suddenly, the house gets bigger, the cars get more expensive, and the toy collection expands (see figure 16.11).

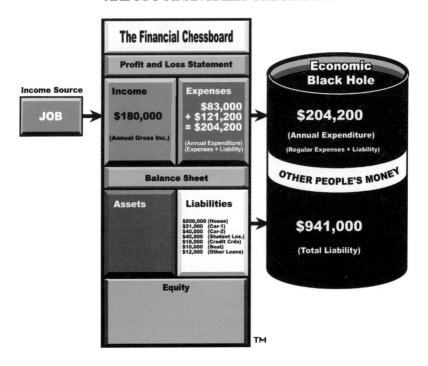

Fig 16.11

Granted, your personal situation may not resemble this outcome exactly. Nonetheless, as a group, we consistently spend roughly 20 percent more than we make regardless of income, a condition that poses serious challenges for anyone who hopes to achieve financial success.

Assets

An *asset* is one of the most misunderstood items in the world of finance, particularly for the average American. People buy jewelry, cars, houses, boats, and similar items on credit, thinking that they're buying assets.

But not all so-called investments are considered assets. The definition of an asset is simple: it's a product or commodity that produces income continuously. In other words, if it doesn't produce income, it doesn't qualify as an asset, unless, it's an expensive piece of jewelry that's completely paid for and appreciating in value. Another way to look at this is that if a *liability* is known to take away money from you each month. An asset does the opposite. It brings money back to you in the form of income.

For example, a business venture procured through a loan from a bank (liability) could be considered an asset if the operation generates a positive cash flow. The same is true for any other commercial property. However, if these commercial enterprises produce no positive cash flow, they fall in the liability category.

This is one of the main reasons why your residence is a liability instead of an asset. It generates no monthly, quarterly, or annual income. Yet over the years, the banking and real-estate industry have done a good job in convincing us that a house is an asset. The only way to make it appear as an asset is by encouraging the public to focus on the potential gains: the *appreciated value* of the house and the *tax write-off* at the end of the year. These are the two main reasons why some people buy houses instead of renting them.

Yet both of these potential gains are unpredictable. They are what I call *conditional* benefits. First, the mortgage interest deduction is a privilege given by law, which can be revoked or changed at any time. As soon as lawmakers find themselves in a bind for cash, Congress can simply manipulate the real estate tax laws in its favor, forcing us to reconsider the housing issue. Furthermore, while it lasts, we have no evidence that homeowners are getting wealthy at the end of the year as a result of a tax write-off. Are you? Or do you find yourself struggling to make mortgage payments instead?

The second issue is that you're assuming that just because you purchase a house that its value will automatically increase. If you think that way, you may want to revisit the late 1980s and early 1990s. As a result of the Tax Reform Act of 1986 and defense cutbacks following the Persian Gulf War of 1991, Southern California property values plummeted by 18 percent, an unfortunate situation for people who were holding residential and commercial properties.

One of the biggest threats to the real estate industry is a rise in unemployment. When people's jobs are unstable or when they get laid off, they're reluctant to make large purchases such as houses and other big-ticket items. Besides, many of them may not be able to qualify simply because they have no income. In this type of situation, real estate demand tends to slow down, causing a corresponding price reduction.

This is not a new thing. Property values fluctuate all the time. But if you're not in the market to buy or sell houses, you probably won't notice the difference. When you become a homeowner, however, the situation becomes more real. Suddenly, you could be forced to sell your property in an economic downswing, causing you to accept a lower price than you anticipated.

On the flip side of the coin, assume that everything goes well in your real estate experience, the value of your house increased, and you have $60,000 in equity (see figure 16.12).

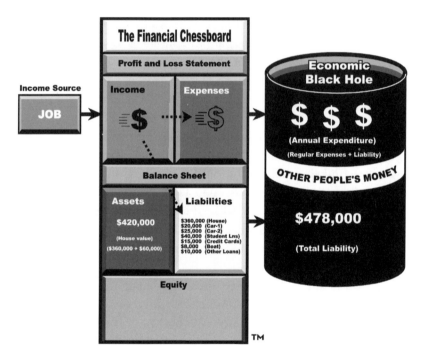

Fig. 16.12

What do you do in this situation? You may think that this money belongs to you. But does it? The truth is, you can't count on it because you never truly own the money. Consider the following:

- If you're unable to maintain your mortgage payment for one reason or the other, and your lien holder forecloses on the property, the equity in house will quickly disappear. You won't see it.

- If you use the equity in the house to pay off debts, improve the house, go on vacation, or send children to college, you'll actually increase your *liability*. This portion of money becomes a debt because it doesn't belong to you in the first place.
- If you sell the house and walk away with $60,000 profit, you may end up with some cash in your pocket, but you end up with a different kind of problem. You're homeless.
- And if you decide to buy another house in the same locality, you may need the $60,000 or more as a down payment on your next purchase. If your property increased in value, so did your neighbors'. Therefore, the gains on your property automatically become a wash.

Do you get the picture? The bottom line? The appreciated value of your house will generally always stay in the house. Consequently, it should never be counted as part of your wealth because the day you tamper with it, you will most likely create additional debt, jeopardizing your situation even more.

What we see instead is that your house, as well as your cars, are assets to the bank or lien holders. Your mortgage and car payments automatically turn into monthly income to your lien holders (see figure 16.13).

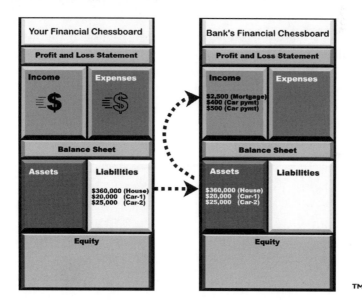

Fig. 16.13

In that case, for the next thirty years, or for as long as you choose to stay in the house, you will be obligated to maintain this financial arrangement.

Equity

The *equity* section of *The Financial Chessboard* is nothing more than a summation of your wealth, an evaluation sheet, or your score card. The amount presented in this block could be either positive or negative, giving you a sense of financial *progression* or *regression*. To illustrate, we need to continue our analysis with the financial model.

But first, it's necessary to emphasize that wealth is not measured by an individual's income but rather by an individual's *net worth*. A person could generate an income in excess of $10,000 a month, for instance. Yet if none of it is kept, the individual may never attain financial success. The same is true for any level of income.

Let's assume that your financial situation resembles the scenario in figure 16.14. Your house has appreciated in value, and you're banking on the increase as part of your wealth. As such, your *net worth* adds up to a negligible $4,850. This is the measure of your wealth despite the fact that you have hundreds of thousands of dollars floating between your asset and liability squares.

In this illustration, If you happen to be in your early twenties, a *net worth* of $4,850 may not appear to be a big problem. Most people at your age have a tendency to feel that they'll have plenty of opportunities to expand their wealth.

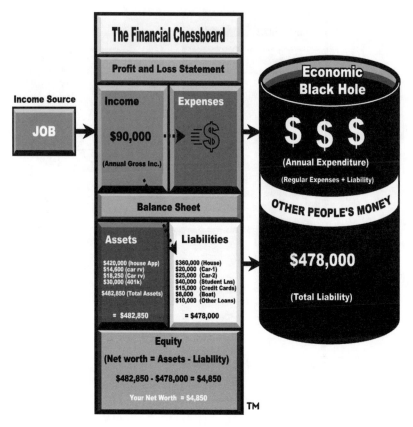

Fig. 16.14

On the other hand, if you're between forty to fifty years old, and your situation looks like this, you have reason to be alarmed. Again, based on the *Life Cycle Expectation Timeline,* between the ages of forty-five and fifty-four, your *net worth* should be approximately $300,000, an amount that could be represented in both liquid and hard assets. Well, it seems like you have a long way to go.

But as bad as this may appear to be at this late stage in life, it can be worse. You happen to be in the black, a positive sign. Many Americans can't say the same thing because they have a net worth of less than zero—that is, even after counting for the *unreliable* appreciated value in the house. For example, many of my client's situations resemble the condition in figure 16.15.

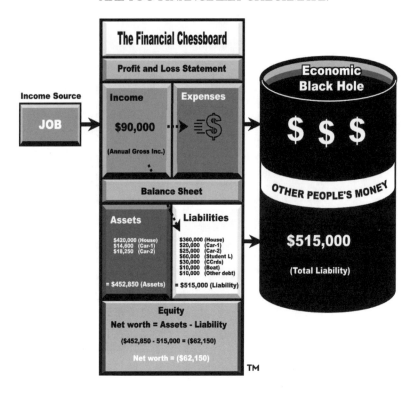

Fig. 16.15

Clearly, there is no wealth in this equation worth mentioning. Here, the negative equity is only $62,150. But many times, the sum is in the hundreds of thousands of dollars. This condition poses a major threat to any individual who hopes to retire comfortably.

People who find themselves in this predicament have actually lost control over the financial affairs. Initially, they thought they were building wealth when, in fact, they were continually increasing their liabilities. With each purchase, they dropped deeper in debt, a condition that's likely to spiral down into a financial crisis. Unfortunately, it's only a matter of time before the game comes to an end, bringing everything to a halt.

The sad part of this critical financial situation is that millions of Americans are in a similar condition but are not aware of it. Part of the problem is that people don't take the time to find out about their net worth. And in some case, they really don't want to know how badly they're doing. Many of my clients, for instance, were shocked to realize that they were doing so poorly, overall, in spite of their handsome incomes.

When it becomes apparent that we're sinking deeper in debt, we begin to act in predictable ways. Those who rent try to find assistance through debt consolidation loans, debt management services, or additional employment. Those of us who have houses take a more sophisticated approach. We use the appreciated value in the house by adding a second or third mortgage on the property or by refinancing the first mortgage.

Either way, the results are the same. Debt is debt wherever or however it's created. The other issue is that it doesn't go away easily. So in a real way, neither the homeowner nor the non-homeowner has accomplished anything positive. Most likely, they have either moved the debt from one place to another or have aggravated their financial situation with more debt.

If you're a homeowner, here is a typical scenario you may experience: you've accumulated about $30,000 debt on three or four credit cards. In the last four years, you've been trying to get rid of it, but the balance keeps getting larger each year. Looking at all your options, you decided to take a second mortgage on the house to pay off the debt.

Since you're borrowing against the equity on the property, you took out an extra $4,000 for a vacation that's long over due. After adding roughly $3,000 of loan processing fees, the total amount came up to $37,000.

When you received the money, you honored your commitment by paying off the credit card debt. At this point, you're totally excited about your situation. You have an upcoming vacation right around the corner, and the pressure from your credit card debt is finally wiped away.

But wait. Have you solved your problem? The answer is, "no." In fact, you've complicated your situation even further. Realistically, you've changed the dynamics of your financial situation, but you haven't noticed the cost (see figure 16.16). It's true that your credit card debt is gone, or so it seems, but you now have two mortgages: one for $360,000, and the other for $37,000.

So, actually, the credit card debt is still there. You've simply swept the dirt from one corner of the house to the next. As a result, you now have a second mortgage, adding more risk to your residence: two lien holders instead of one. Furthermore, you still have a good portion of your old debt remaining, bringing your total liability to $522,000, not counting the interest.

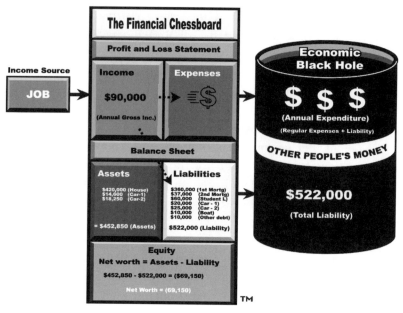

Fig. 16.16

Notice also that your income and the appreciated value of the house have basically remained flat. These signs suggest that you may be in a sluggish economy that could last months or even years. Meanwhile, your net worth has actually dropped, making you poorer than prior to initiating the second mortgage.

At this point, your economy is on the verge of collapsing completely. You have no cash on hand for emergencies, no more collateral for additional debt, no assets that produce income, and no equity worth mentioning. Translation: if everything you claim to have was to be sold to pay off all your debt, you'd still be owing roughly $69,150. As mentioned earlier, this another way to visualize a *financially checkmate* position.

What you do from this point is predictable. Since you have no cash reserve and all your income is consumed by regular expenses and liability obligations, you'll gradually recreate the credit card debt you just eradicated. It's as though we feel that unless we're madly spending money on credit cards, we're not making progress, an attitude that habitually puts us further and further behind financially.

What happens if we increase your asset by $50,000? Let's assume that you have 401k retirement plan totaling fifty thousand dollars. "This ought to mean something," you say. Positively, yes, it does. Notwithstanding, when we plug this amount in your asset square, your situation still looks bleak, meaning, you still have less than zero equity (see figure 16.17).

Sorry. When your liability is this high, it takes a lot of assets to make a positive difference in your favor. Notice that $50,000 is hardly changing anything. When you do the math, you're still in the negative.

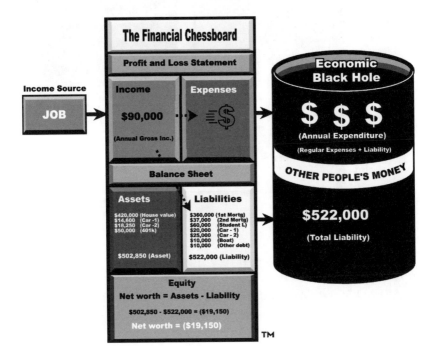

Fig. 16.17

There is yet another possibility worth considering. Let's suppose that your situation doesn't come close to what we've described so far. Realistically, you could be doing a lot better. The value of your house has gone up to a $150,000, bringing the total appraised value to $510,000 (see figure 16.18). Furthermore, your retirement accounts have a combined total of $100,000. As such, you feel secure and comfortable about your situation. Well, let's see what happens in your accounting system.

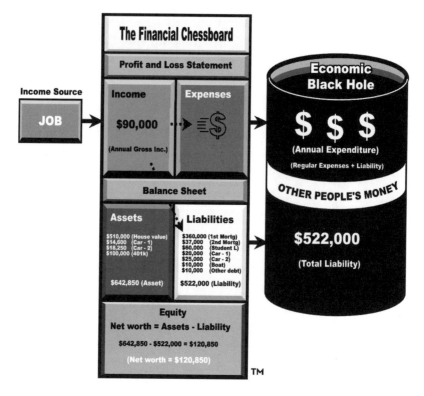

Fig. 16.18

Looking at figure 16.18, you have obviously improved your situation. Your assets have increased $642,850, bringing your net worth to a total of $120,850. At this point, you may be excited. However, it's a little too early for that because based on what we've discussed so far, your situation is still unstable. Here is why:

1. You shouldn't depend on the appreciated value of the house as wealth because, as we mentioned earlier, it really doesn't exist.
2. You've borrowed $37,000 from the $150,000 to pay off credit card debts. Any additional borrowing will increase your debt load, reducing your net worth even more.
3. The only tangible asset you can claim is your retirement account ($100,000).
4. Assuming you don't increase your debt and want to maintain your current lifestyle during retirement, the $100,000 will last no more than a couple of years.

Food for Thought

Perhaps you and your spouse have a combined annual income of $90,000. This level of revenue suggests that you're a middle-class American family. Since you are buying a house, we can also assume that you're in your late thirties or mid-forties. If you find yourself struggling from paycheck to paycheck each year, aren't you a bit curious as to what's happening? My guess is that you are, like many of the clients I've seen.

The interesting thing is, the majority of Americans are experiencing financial insufficiency. That includes people who are commanding a high six-figure income as well. Yet few will admit to it because the situation is utterly embarrassing.

Where is your money going each year? The answer is simple. Notice that most of your money leaves your hands through the liability square of your financial chessboard and into the economic black hole (see figure 16.19).

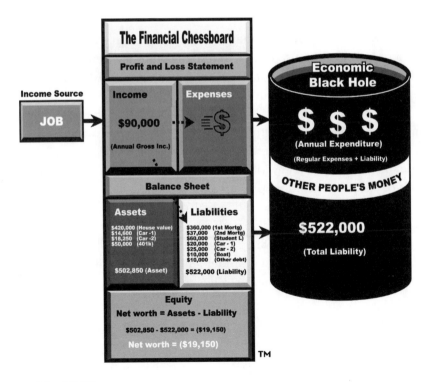

Fig. 16.19

When this happens, other people are profiting from your labor. In that case, year after year, you're simply working to put profits in other people's pockets or bank accounts. Those who benefit the most are the ones who loan you the money to buy all the possessions you to have. These individuals or banks are standing by each month, waiting to collect interest payments from you.

Obviously, as long as you stay in this situation, you will forever be indebted to your creditors, making them wealthy instead of you. Unless this is your intention, you must pull yourself from this type of financial quagmire and vow never to be controlled like this in the future.

Meanwhile, if you find the foregoing information to be disturbing, you shouldn't blame yourself too much. You're simply a victim of the economic culture designed to keep you broke. *First,* the culture provided you little or no financial training while growing up. *Second,* it encouraged you to live for today and forget about tomorrow. *Third,* it persuaded you to buy things on credit, making believe that you were building wealth. And *fourth,* when you got trapped by debt, it discarded you, conveying the idea that you're weak, untrusting, unreliable, and pathetic.

Knowing this, my hope is that you will change the way you conduct business. Vow to allow no one, including the culture, to manipulate you without your good judgment. With this attitude, you'll begin to take control of your financial future.

Incidentally, what you've just read in this chapter is the way most Americans understand wealth is to be created. But as you've noticed when the numbers are added, the sum is adversely affecting the individual or the home. Meanwhile, the economy as a whole does well as a result of excessive spending primarily on credit.

On the other hand, the individual struggles while trying to stay afloat financially. This cultural path to success is a survival root, one that encourages people to live on the brink of disaster. As a result, those of us who desire to be financially independent should find other means for doing so. The next chapter provides some recommendations.

CHAPTER 17

Winning the Money Game

B ecoming a chess master, or developing any level of proficiency in the game of chess, is not easy. A person first has to have the desire to be good at the game. From that point, the individual needs to be mentally prepared to exercise an incredible amount of time and patience to learn it. With consistent determination, over time, he or she will have developed a set of skills, knowledge, and specific strategies to beat the opponent. This is usually accomplished after spending years reading about chess, watching others play the game, dedicating time for practice, and having the willingness to lose, again and again, to a stronger opponent.

Winning the game of money or becoming financially independent requires the same type of commitment. First, you need to have the desire to be wealthy. Without a "hunger" or an absolute passion to become financially free, everything else is pointless. Once this is established, you need to utilize self-discipline and patience long enough to attain your goal. Initially, much of your time will be spent acquiring three basic components necessary to building wealth: (1) *knowledge* about money—basic money management and investment strategies, (2) *experience* with the commodity—financial skills to know what works in our economic system and what to avoid, and (3) *money* itself—yours or that of others.

As you take on this challenge, keep in mind that wealth doesn't automatically find people and make them rich. The phenomenon gradually becomes part of you as you work to make it happen. Once a plan of success is put in motion, you simply need to remain committed to the end. Then little by little, the mundane routine you perform each day takes you closer to your goal. Sometimes, you don't even see the small changes as they occur. Then suddenly, you're living your dream.

While it's true that this event happens sooner for some than others, everyone must pay a price for success. In addition to a cash investment, the process always requires some struggle, patience, commitment, and time. In fact, more often than not, this is where many people fail in business. For example, it could be much easier for someone to invest thousands of dollars in a project than to exercise long-term *commitment* to see it to the end. Yet, it is the personal attributes that are crucial to long-term success. They help an individual gain respect for riches or possessions and learn to appreciate them.

Another consideration to building wealth is that it hardly ever comes to people who are content with a job and see nothing beyond their career. In previous chapters, we spoke of the economic entrapment—the income restriction that employers place on employees. Because salaries and wages are controlled by the economy itself, most employees get just enough pay for their daily survival. One needs to break away from income restrictions in order to experience an abundance of money—much more that what the bills and debts require on a monthly basis. Money that's not needed for daily survival can then be invested for greater income leverage.

If you're enjoying your current job and don't desire to have more money, you're obviously content. Therefore, you don't need to do anything except to maintain the status quo. On the other hand, if you have come to dislike the idea of people taking advantage of you financially, you need to change your strategy, much of which may require a new outlook on life. In other words, you must be mentally prepared to change your personal conduct or way of doing business if you want better results. Realistically, you cannot expect a different set of circumstances with old habits.

One of the first things you must consider doing is to avoid the influence of the masses. The way of the majority simply doesn't work, mainly because when too many people try to do the same thing, the only reasonable expectation is mediocrity—nothing better. Therefore, you need to observe the behavior of the masses and do just the opposite.

Case in point, you can't wake up at six o'clock in the morning, have breakfast, get on the freeway an hour or so later, and expect to avoid rush-hour traffic. This is unreal in any major metropolitan area in the United States. If you want to minimize or avoid the rush-hour madness, you need to be ahead of the game, leaving before the period when the majority of people wake up, do their morning chores, and get on the freeway. Otherwise, you'll continue to be stuck in traffic while fighting to get to your destination.

Remember, every business, regardless of the industry, is concerned about its own success and not yours. That includes your financial planner; your real-estate agent, broker, or banker; your credit card companies; your boss; the company you work for; and anyone else.

Knowing this, your decisions should be based on your gut feeling and not on the influences of the media, magazines, or experts. Though you should never turn down wise counsel, nothing is more accurate than your gut feeling, assuming you have enough information to guide you. Chart your own course and don't allow yourself to be influenced or manipulated by others anymore.

You also need to keep in mind that the path to financial prosperity isn't simple. Neither is it popular nor easy. Otherwise, most people would be financially free. It's nice to know, however, that half the joy of attaining financial success is the process of getting there. So enjoy the journey. If you put the time and effort into something that promises a return, and you don't quit, you'll be rewarded in the end.

The Power of Assets

So far, you've attempted to build your empire with the use of credit. By doing so, you kept increasing your liability or debt in the process. You followed this route because that's what the masses have been trained to do. Today, you have less wealth than you expected at your age.

As mentioned in the previous chapter, there is a tiebreaker in this whole financial game. And that is the accumulation of *assets* (see figure 17.1). You'll see why this is so as we continue.

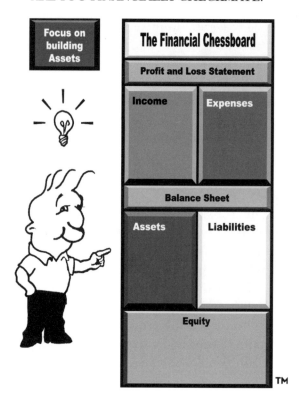

Fig. 17.1

The good news is there are a number of ways of building assets:

The Cash Approach to Assets

The *cash approach* to building assets is nothing more than utilizing cash to generate income. This method focuses on security investments such as government bonds and corporate stocks and bonds. Other options may include mutual funds, precious metals, and so on.

The advantage of using cash to accumulate wealth suggests that you have some control. The fact is, you're actually in a position of lending money instead of borrowing it. As a lender of money, you're poised to collecting interests or dividends as opposed to paying them, giving you some degree of financial leverage. Some cash-asset options are shown in figure 17.2.

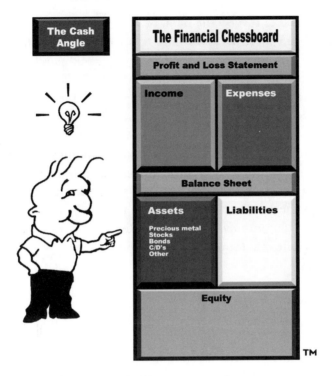

Fig. 17.2

One of the biggest hurdles to building wealth with this option is that few people have cash on hand to invest. In most cases, the economy takes 100 percent of their income each month, leaving them with little or nothing to invest.

These are the same people who usually struggle to make ends meet. More than likely, they've crossed over the boundary lines of their income and ventured deep into the liability quagmire, a condition best described as living beyond your means. Meanwhile, Wall Street remains a mystery, a place where most people believe wealth is created, yet few are able to take advantage of the gold rush.

The people who are able to capitalize on Wall Street or the stock market are those with extra cash. How they got the extra money makes little or no difference, except to assume that they learned how to live within their means. One reasonable explanation is that they permitted the economy to draw from them less than what it provided them, allowing them the opportunity to use the extra cash for building assets.

Your goal is to reverse the habit of living beyond your means. Thus, from this point forward, determine to spend no more than $0.90 on each dollar. In other words, practice living on 90 percent of your income while saving or investing 10 percent.

If you practice this habit, you'll develop three fundamental benefits that are crucial to your financial future:

1. At the end of the year, you will have accumulated some cash in your account, if you remain consistent with the habit,
2. You will learn to live on less than you make, a monumental feat considering your previous habit, and
3. Most importantly, you will have developed a degree of financial discipline that you haven't had, one that will pay huge dividends later.

Consider, for example, that your income falls within the range of what's depicted in figure 17.3. Furthermore, assume that you decide to save or keep 10 percent of your earnings for investments. Notice that the 10 percent you saved actually went into your asset square on the financial chessboard. This money is yours and should be treated as seed money for future growth.

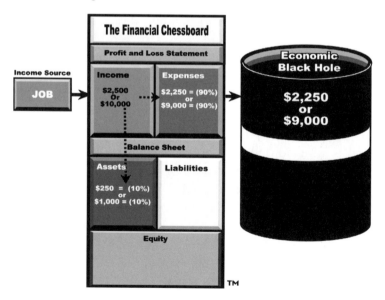

Fig. 17.3

Granted, this formula by itself won't make you wealthy overnight, but it's a good start. In fact, you won't accomplish a great deal of wealth until you're able to master this basic concept. The truth is, this is where the accumulation of wealth begins—a consistent discipline of repeating—a tedious pattern of positive actions.

Bypassing this concept, thinking that you need to have the big bucks to make it work, will cost you dearly. A good friend of mine once said to me, "My business made over one million dollars in revenue last year, but I have no idea where the money went." This honest confession proves that it makes no difference how much money a person makes if he or she ignores the fundamentals of money management, the basis of which starts with saving 10 percent of your earnings.

Learning to master the art of living on 90 percent of your income won't be easy. In fact, this simple concept will challenge the best in you. Three obvious roadblocks will get in your way as you make the attempt to do so:

1. Your old spending habits will flare up. As a result, you may find yourself struggling to keep spending under control and, sometimes, you may lose the fight,
2. You might be overly extended in debt. If that's the case, you must find a way to reduce your debt while scaling back on expenses. Keep cutting back on expenditures until you're able to find a comfortable 10 percent of your income for savings, and
3. You've never had the consistent discipline of putting money away in savings or investments. For some people, this exercise is pure torture. The fact that they can't spend the money "today" becomes a major ordeal much like an addict withdrawing from a fix. You may end up having the same experience.

But nothing mentioned here is impossible. All these challenges can be overcome if you get serious about your financial future. The best way to approach this challenge is to affirm your commitment in resolving this issue. One way to do this is by grabbing yourself by the shirt collar and saying positively, "Buddy, we haven't done this before. It won't be easy, but we're going to make it happen because it's important." It is this type of attitude that will break the habits that have kept you broke to this point.

Another way to look at the situation is, when it comes to spending money, 10 percent of your income will hardly make a notable difference in your lifestyle. In other words, if you can't live on 90 percent of your income and feel that you've got to have the extra 10 percent to complete your fun, food purchases, debt payments, and so on, your condition is hopeless.

Yet with some consistency, 10 percent of your income can go a long way when invested. For instance, assume that your take-home pay is $5,000 a month, ten percent of this amount would be $500. If this money is invested in a mutual fund yielding 10 percent annual return, in ten years, your investment would amount to roughly $103,276.01, if you started at zero.

Now, if you're one of those individuals swamped with debt, saving or investing 10 percent of your income may not be feasible initially. However, you may be able to get the ball rolling with 5 percent. And if this amount is still too much, by golly, put $20 away in your savings each month and leave it there. If you are consistent, the time will come when you'll be able to do better. But whatever you do, don't let your entire paycheck fly through your fingers each month and end up in the economic black hole.

By the way, you're certainly not restricted to saving only 10 percent of your income. You can always do more if you can. This amount is only a recommendation. On the other hand, if you have the capacity to do more, avoid going overboard. Life can be quite boring when too much emphasis is placed on savings. In other words, there are those who save excessively while dressing in rags, eating bread, drinking water, and having no fun. Avoid this problem. Life requires balance and this is certainly true in the case of money management.

Again, the purpose of this discipline is to establish good financial habits and not overnight success. Realistically, accumulating money through savings or investments is one of the slowest methods of achieving financial independence. Since the initial amount of investment for the average person is usually small, one must regard time and the mechanics of compounding interest for a significant change or increase in wealth. Additionally, other complications may arise that, sometimes, thwart or delay the savings plan, making the entire process appear more difficult than it's meant to be.

The Credit Approach to Assets

Believe it or not, you can use credit to build assets. But it has to be *profit-generating* credit as opposed to the *consumable* form. For what it's worth, most Americans are more familiar with *consumable* credit for obvious reasons. We use this kind of credit for food, education, and possessions.

In some situations, the interest rate on *consumable* credit can be low. Rates on first mortgages, car loans, and student loans come to mind as examples. Most of the time, however, the rates are high. Credit cards serve as a good example in this situation. Some rates are as high as 25 percent on regular purchases. But regardless of the rates, the end result is the same. The borrower usually ends up with a cul-de-sac arrangement, meaning, once the money is spent, the borrower has the obligation to pay the note in full without any additional benefits.

Unfortunately, for many of us, this is where our financial problems begin. Depending on the size and length of the loan, we fall short of meeting the obligated arrangement. Most of the time, we end up defaulting on the loan contract, subsequently creating multiple problems for ourselves.

The *profit-generating credit,* on the other hand, is different. One can borrow money to open a business of any type and profit from the extra income. As long as the business keeps making money, part of the revenue can be used to make monthly payments on the loan while the rest stays in the business. The business portion can then be used as reserve, inventory, and owners' salaries. Hence, a profit-generating machine.

Profit-generating credit can be used for any type of business. However, the ones that work best for our purposes are those that require minimal time and supervision from the owner. For instance, a product business is ideal for this type of situation because once the product is created, if marketed properly, it can generate an endless stream of cash flow or revenue for the owner.

Unfortunately, picking the right type of product business is not always easy. The choices stretch from *A* to *Z* in various categories, making the selection somewhat challenging for the creative mind. For instance, you could establish a publishing business, selling only magazines, books (new or used), various newspapers, and so on; a computer-software enterprise, developing financial, legal, or security applications; a real estate venture in residential or commercial properties; a gasoline station; a flower shop; and the list goes on.

For accounting purposes, figure 17.4 illustrates the position of a business that produces excess revenue. That means, a business that generates enough income to pay for the debt and some money leftover. Notice that the capital invested in the business is borrowed money which is placed in the liability square. Yet the business itself is placed in the asset square, that is, as long as it produces profits.

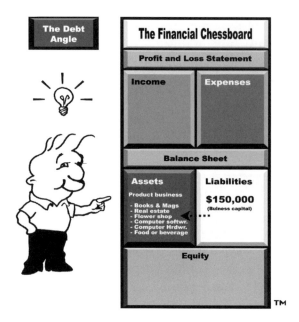

Fig. 17.4

When thinking of a business, the initial steps usually conjures up the need for capital or seed money. Yet that should be the last thing on your list. While it's always best to having your own start-up capital, finding money is usually not a problem. Venture capitalists are always ready and able to support a good plan. The same is true for the Small Business Administration (SBA) as well as family members with extra cash. So your concern should not necessarily be on the need for capital, but rather on finding the right type of business.

Why get into business in the first place? Well, the reasons vary from one individual to the next. But for most people, it's a matter of personal control, a sense of destiny, freedom, or power. Most importantly, the need for money—lots of it. A profitable business is the quickest way of becoming wealthy in this country. It is through business ventures that most wealthy Americans have become financially successful. And the potential for great success still looms at the horizon for those who have the courage to get it. You could be the next wealthy person in this country if you desire. The level of wealth, of course, is left up to you.

One of the great marvels of starting a business is that you can do so while working for your current employer. As long as you maintain your commitment to the company, no harm is done. On the other hand, you must be cautious with the gray area. You cannot allow your personal interest to infringe on your employer's time or interest. Otherwise, you could be held liable for conflict of interest.

On the flip side of the coin, you could be involved in a business that requires your total involvement initially. That means, you would consider yourself an employee of your business, getting paid just like anyone else who works for you.

Either way, whether you're employed by your own company or working for someone else, you must wait until your assets can produce enough revenue to quit your job or pull back from a full-time position in your company. If implemented properly, it will eventually happen, giving you enough money to pay all expenses and liabilities and having money leftover for other things (see figure 17.5).

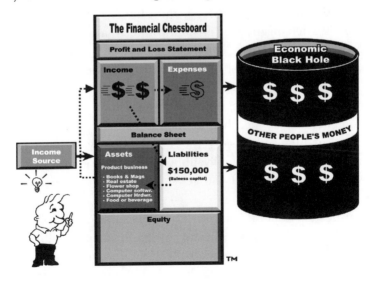

Fig. 17.5

When your assets get to the point of generating solid income, you may not need your job anymore unless, of course, you want to continue working for someone else. But notice that the job is removed from the equation, and instead, revenue or income is flowing from your assets into the income square of your accounting system. This is the type of equation that is primarily responsible for making a lot of Americans wealthy, and the same technique is available to you.

The interesting thing is, once you get going, there is no stopping. Each idea or business venture lends itself as a catapult for additional opportunities. As soon as you get established in one enterprise, your creative mind continues to search for additional ways to make more money. As such, you'll get plenty of opportunities to invest additional dollars in worthwhile ventures, diversifying yourself even further. Some of ventures may be germane to your original idea, and others could be totally unrelated. The idea is to spread yourself wide enough to anchor your financial interests as deep as possible.

The idea is, business or job, you never want to find yourself relying on one source of income. Your financial or economic interest remains continually vulnerable when you place yourself in that position. The good news is, while the job limits your capacity to generate huge sums of money, businesses provide unlimited income opportunities.

As mentioned earlier, a product business is more conducive to this type of arrangement. Nevertheless, the same technique can be employed in a service business. If erected properly, a service-type venture could provide the same set of benefits as the product venture (see figure 17.6). As long as you are not directly involved in the day-to-day operation of the business, you should do just as well.

But if you are spending twelve to fifteen-hour days in a business trying to generate income, this situation is no better than working for someone else-unless the arrangement is temporary. In fact, in some cases, it's worse because your livelihood rests squarely on your shoulders. And heaven forbids, if you get sick or injured. There goes your income.

Do avoid this pitfall if you can. The idea is to hire people (managers and other employees) to run the operation while you, the business owner, oversees the operation and collects the revenue. If this equation is in place, it makes no difference what kind of service you provide. You will eventually produce the revolving-income situation, similar to that of a product business (see figure 17.6).

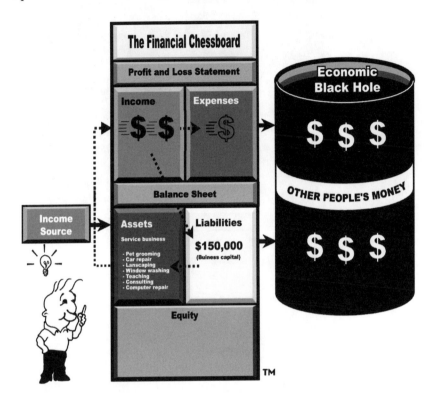

Fig. 17.6

The Cash and Credit Approach to Assets

Money has a unique way of building on itself when used properly. Like the roots of a plant, it has the ability to spread in various directions for strength. So as you think about your financial strategy, one way to look at the whole game is to see yourself building wealth using both the *cash* and *debt* concepts simultaneously, a method used by the rich over and over again (see figure 17.7).

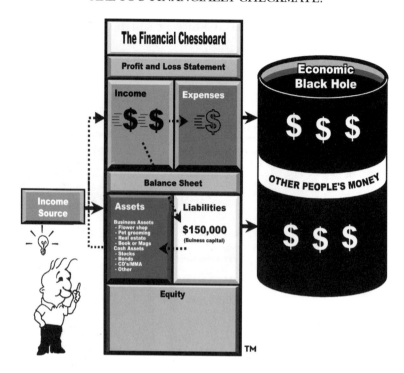

Fig 17.7

Unless you have a huge amount of cash on hand, the game starts with your hard assets (businesses) generating a healthy amount of cash flow. After handling all immediate expenses and liabilities, you simply channel some of your reserve into security investments. This is where you'll need the expertise of a financial planner and accountant (highly recommended for best results). Their job is to guide you into various aspects of investments including tax planning, retirement preparation, estate planning, and so on.

Initially, set no limits at the top. Allow your businesses and cash investments to expand as big as you can imagine. Conversely, settle for nothing less than a $1 million *net worth*. Here is why. Assume you have a net worth of a $1 million, and most of it is invested in government securities, yielding roughly 5 percent annual return. Assume also that you have no other income, and you are drawing out approximately $3,000 per month to maintain your lifestyle during retirement, under these conditions, $1 million will last forever. Anything more is simply icing on the cake.

Figure 17.8 depicts a particular scenario. Keep in mind that all figures are fictitious or otherwise arbitrary. Also, remember that the focus here is not necessarily to teach you the fine points of accounting but rather to demonstrate a cash-flow process.

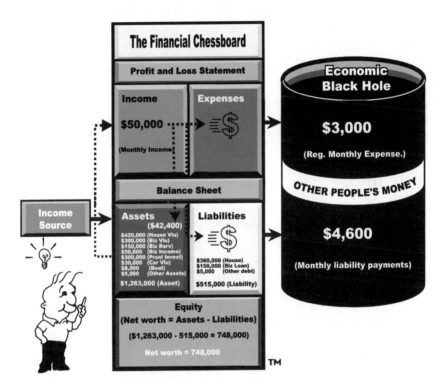

Fig. 17.8

To begin, notice that a bank loan can be procured to buy assets, which may ultimately generate income. A second mortgage on your house can be used in the same capacity. Now, imagine that your business is generating $50,000 each month, a sum big enough to pay all monthly expenses, including liabilities. Furthermore, imagine after taking care of all expenses, you have roughly $42,000 to reinvest in the business and for personal use. Any similar scenario will do just fine. But that's the idea.

With this much money, it's easy to eradicate some debt completely. You can wipe away credit card balances, student loans, car loans, and boat loans as shown in our model. Your house mortgage remains optional.

At this point, the majority of *consumable* debt is paid in full, limiting the risks to your personal and professional assets as well as the rest of your financial interests.

Notice that the majority of your income stays with you instead of going out into the economic black hole. The resulting benefit is an increase in your asset base, an amount doubling the amount of your liability (see figure 17.8)

Finally, based on all these financial dynamics, your score card shows that you're, positively, $748,000 wealthy. Now, imagine that this is only the beginning.

The financial model depicted in figure 17.8 should be your ultimate financial goal. With this view, your reach is unlimited.

Your Move

At this point, I have no idea how you feel or what you're thinking. But my concern for you is that you remove yourself from being *Financially Checkmate*. This immobilized position is characterized by the following conditions:

- You find yourself living from paycheck to paycheck,
- You can't afford to loose your job because your empire will crumble in two or three months,
- Most of your possessions are purchased on credit,
- Your retirement plan is woefully lacking funds,
- And you're nervous about your financial security,

If you find yourself relating to any part of the above descriptions, you need to start your financial strategy over again before things get worse. My hope is that you have been empowered by the information from this book, and you're ready to take steps to change your life for the better.

As you start building your wealth, life will begin to change. Not only will you be solving your money problems once and for all, but you'll also start experiencing a sense of freedom, control, and power, the things we all want even when left unspoken.

From this point on, decide to disregard limiting beliefs and values regarding money. Money is and will always be a neutral commodity, meaning, in the hands of those who are malicious and bent to doing evil, money will appear to be evil. Conversely, those who are honest and caring, money will appear to be good. So it's all a matter of perspective.

Therefore, don't be afraid of money. Neither should you be timid or apologetic in conversation or demeanor for having the desire to be rich. Remember, most of us want to be financially independent. Some people simply have more guts than others to admit it in public.

Instead, learn to appreciate and respect money. You do so by increasing your *knowledge* and *experience* about this precious commodity. Part of this familiarity is learning to manage it well by creating a good balance between spending and saving. When you do, money will reward you in ways that you haven't experienced.

Part of becoming successful is to imagine great possibilities. Allow yourself the freedom to dream without limits. Then pursue your dreams or imaginations with passion. Meanwhile, refuse to be pushed, pulled, and prodded by others who are not interested in your success.

So until we meet again. I wish you success and Godspeed.